Also by BRUCE WEBER

POETRY

These Poems Are Not Pretty (with Jan McLaughlin)
How the Poem Died
The First Time I Had Sex with T.S. Eliot

ANTHOLOGIES

Downtown Poets Anthology (co-editor)

ART HISTORY

Homage to the Square:
Picturing Washington Square, 1890-1965
The Heart of the Matter:
The Still Lifes of Marsden Hartley

CD

Bruce Weber's No Chance Ensemble:
Let's Dine Like Jack Johnson Tonight

POETIC JUSTICE

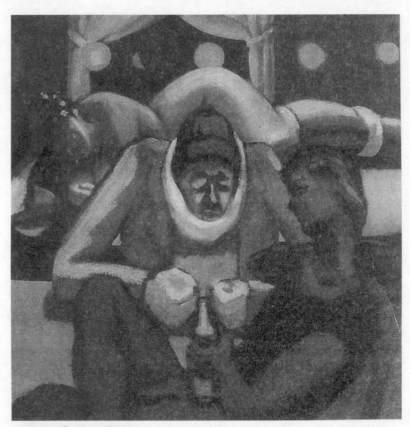

Joanne Pagano Weber
Man and Woman
Oil on canvas
14½ x 14½ inches

POETIC JUSTICE

Bruce Weber

with artwork by
**Arturo Rodríguez &
Joanne Pagano Weber**

IKON
New York, New York

FOR MOM

Work from this collection has appeared in the following
publications: *A Gathering of the Tribes, Chronogram, Hart,
Stained Sheets, Tamarind.*

ISBN:0-945368-08-9
Library of Congress Control Number: 2004102895
First Edition
Printed in Canada by AGMV Marquis

Cover painting detail: Joanne Pagano Weber, *Man and Woman.*

*With special thanks to Joanne Pagano Weber, Susan Sherman
and Paul Pines.*

IKON
151 First Avenue, #46
New York, NY 10003
www.hometown.aol.com/IkonInc
IkonInc@aol.com

CONTENTS

THE SPACE BETWEEN TREES

THE WOMAN WITH THE VIDEO CAMERA

POETIC JUSTICE

ILLUMINATIONS
Paintings by Arturo Rodríguez

THE SPACE BETWEEN TREES

GUESSING GAME POEM

it's
bigger
than the bread basket of the wealthy
proper as a bostonian in a henry james novel
idiosyncratic
as
a
life preserver on the titanic
it
laughs
all the way to its pauper's grave
it's
a
shadow
recalled in a poem by rimbaud
something recorded on film
something exposed to sunlight
something allowed to disappear
under the auspices
of the cia
it needs to be kept
in a tightly clasped envelope
it's impossible to draw clearly
it's blurry like a heavy snowfall
it's
ridiculous
as a bad comic's timing
it's
soggier
than
an alcoholic stupor
it's
periwinkle blue

it's
sent in a bee's mouth
from blossom to blossom
cherish
it
like a favorite old sweater
suck it
in your nostrils
like a snort of cocaine
chill
out
with
it
close the door
and
make love with it
now that you're aware of its rhythm
consider
it
one of the seven wonders of the ancient world
run your fingers
across its grain
huddle close to it
without brushing it off
without shrugging your shoulders
be
humble
before
it
s
salutation
welcoming
you

in
to
its
cave
its
hive
its
coffin

WHEN HERKOMER SPOKE

when herkomer spoke seagulls
flew around his head
like a halo
and
cowboys drank a toast
to the last of the
buffalo
when herkomer spoke
someone whistled the melody
to old man river
someone hailed a taxi
with a hundred dollar bill
someone shuddered
like a toaster
coughing
up
burnt
rye
bread
when herkomer spoke
i whispered like a leaf being watered
i walked into a labyrinth carrying a compass
i stood on my head and delivered
the emancipation proclaimation
when herkomer spoke
comets whizzed by
like an orchestra led by count basie
and
sparks flew from the head of medusa
when herkomer spoke
i put away childish weapons
i recited blake
i lay down in a field with lambs

i slept like the baby krishna
when herkomer spoke
i wound up my little boy's top
and
watched
it

```
        s
     g     p
  n           i
     i   n
        n
```

SIT WITH KANDINSKY

sit with kandinsky and hold a conversation about
pre-world war I munich or berlin or paris. open up your
third eye and become kandinsky's brush. imagine the
drips and lines filling his canvas. a netherworld extending
its reach beyond the secret meanings of color, like a
mandala, like the inner life of a flower, like climbing to the
top of the himalayas. tell kandinsky you want to become a
blur in one of his paintings. a thin membrane consuming
light and air. your skin a resonant surface illuminated by
fire. disappear in the swift climb of a brushstroke. the
c-shaped form teetering on the brink of combustion. feel
the wind through your hair. through your skin. through your
imagination. don't be afraid to go play in someone else's
garden. your body stretching over the linen surface.
obeying the rules of chaos theory. choosing a destination
in time in space in the fourth dimension. becoming a
curve. becoming spirit. becoming the thrust of a diagonal
entering the ear of heaven.

"You enshrine things that you cannot explain"
—Rev. Nick Morris, Oklahoma City, The New York Times

here is the place to pile things. memories of strange
couplings in out-of-the-way italian hotels. glimmers of
extraterrestrial light peeking through venetian blinds. the
hesitations of a hand moving along a thigh to the paydirt
of love and god and resurrection. throw on this place the
mattress set fire to by the abused child striking back at
daddy's habits. sling on it the uzi still steaming from an
out-of-control night at the amusement park. place on it the
diaries of your growing up years in the orphanage you
always got left behind in because you demanded too many
kisses. convince your best friends to lug in the car you
abandoned in savannah haunted by bats and moss and
hooting owls. pile on it the ashes of the dead/the dust
collecting in shoe boxes/the residue of out of the way
places unturned since 1957. cast off the spooky
photograph you bought for a quarter in a flea market in
lisbon/the pocket watch singing old man river when you
open it slowly/the intimacy we shared on a balcony
overlooking the spanish steps when i was proceeding
through the latter stages of adolescence. this is a shrine
to unexplainable things flickering in the night. dazzling
back roads of the mind with penumbras of candles.
defying wild west speculations/academic reinterpretations
/oddball cures/and pauses before open windows by
men and women teetering on the scale of their lives.

MY GREAT AUNT SUSAN SEWED
THIS CRAZY QUILT

my great aunt susan sewed this crazy quilt during her newlywed years following the civil war. there's an engraved picture of general ulysses s. grant waving his hand for the coming election, and poor abe lincoln riding through springfield, illinois on a white horse when he was a boy. many of the surfaces are marked with the initials of her friends and kinsmen, tokens of her affection and regard for the people who looked after her in her growing up years, when she wasn't able to outdistance herself from being fragile, like this pale advertisement for a porcelain doll. there's the image of the mail order wedding dress she sent for from london, made of lace sewn by the hands of young girls in a milltown south of liverpool. there's the dried remnants of the white gardenia she wore when she said yes to james arlington at the reformed church up the road. across the quilt's northernmost territory are the faces great aunt susan sewed of her little sisters and brothers, running through the forest in summer picking wild blackberries and mushrooms. you can tell by the worn and turned over edges, like leaves falling from maple trees in autumn, that one day this quilt stopped blossoming like a garden through the threads of her tender bones. yes this crazy quilt's passed down through every generation of my family. from great aunt susan's niece emily to her daughter adelia to my mother louise. now i hang it over my bed and look up to it like it's a constellation of where i come from. it's been touched and caressed and loved by every woman of my family. it's withstood every wind howling through this town's long hard story, surviving the closing of the mill and the fickleness of the visitors who once flocked to the lakeshore in summertime. and i just stare into the spaces in between each string and picture, looking for some trace of my great aunt susan's spirit, rising above the legacy she's left behind the women of her family, like a hop, a skip and a jump over each rock that runs along the creek south of town, and every night i cross myself and say a little prayer for great aunt susan so she knows just how much she's been missed.

THE COMPLEX SENTENCE

the complex sentence went on vacation, becoming a hiccup,
an erasure, a semi-colon. the complex sentence giving up
its itching, its wiggling, its redundancies, like a lifer at san
quentin welcoming god into his life. the complex sentence
no longer pretended it was in love with henry james' novels
because it was fed up with driving slowly to out of the way
places in quest of a subject, a predicate, and a *raison
d'etre*. the complex sentence went on the road for a literary
tour of american bookstores reading from its safely
published ifs & buts & as well as. satisfying the stuffed
shirts coming in quest of an epiphany at the end of a long
walk across the burial ground of the sentence. like a buxom
blond standing on the corner of hollywood and vine awaiting
redemption. the complex sentence snipping at the heels
of the barking chihuahua, clipping at the deranged hairdo of
the receptionist polishing her nails, stripping away
the excess fodder stuffing itself in the sentence like a pita
sandwich. making the world a more digestible place to be
a sheet metal worker, stilt walker, or poet.

LIE TO ME

lie
to
me
whisper in my ear
that i'm adorable
that i'm sexy
that you want to fuck me
that i take your breath away
that i leave you sighing
leave you moaning
leave you hyperventilating
yeah
lie
to
me
tell me i'm mr. wonderful
tell me i'm irresistible
tell me i'm dreamy
yeah
deceive me with words
that won't ever hurt me
that soothe my skin
like a couple of hard slaps
of aftershave lotion
build me up
so i won't ever crumble into destitution
like a shadow of someone
who once had a wife and family
yeah lie to me
make up something
that makes me feel good for a couple of seconds
tell me i'm helpful
tell me i'm handy

tell me i'm hunky
tell me i'm indispensable in an emergency
tell me i'm beefy enough to be your lover
tell me i'm everything you've ever dreamed of
yeah
lie
to
me

EE CUMMINGS' HAT

o
hat
on
ee
cummings'
pumpkin
seed
shaped
head
perched
there
to
accept
the
day
and
what
a
day
hat
can
you
size
up
the
world
the
way
it
wanted
to
be
among
the

moderns
stripping
language
of
its
polite
order
sanding
off
the
quaintness
of
queen
victoria's
gilded
century?
o
hat
tell me how
a
poem
can
extenuate
the
circumstances
of
grammar's
iron
fisted
rules
with
open
parenthesis
pulling
the
moon

into
the
equationless
room
the
blue
aroma
of
a
space
less
apost
ro
ph
e
?

SARAH GREENWOOD

i water the geraniums in this planter every summer evening when the sun's going down. i'm proud to be a member of the ladies auxiliary in long-standing and good health. that's the monument to the citizens who went off and saved the union. my great grandfather ezekial's name is in the middle of the pack of vermont battalion one hundred and eleven who never came home from pickett's charge. my daughter carolyn and her husband live around the corner with their kids. that's them playing at the top of the hill, pulling their wheelbarrow and falling down. this town square's looking proper since we polished the statue of that soldier standing at attention for a hundred years. he looks like betty gillahan's son chester who went off to fight in the last war. he sent home a photograph of himself standing by his fighter plane smiling and raising his right hand to his brow. that statue's a good luck charm protecting us from any disturbance that might rattle this old new england town. we have to protect what we've gathered or else there's not going to be any america left to breathe in any more. everything passes in a cycle so we'll still be waving at each other on the road when it does. maybe i'll see you tomorrow. i'm here with the setting sun to welcome anyone i can.

SHOESHINE

shoeshine, shoeshine, he said, so i sat on his homemade
soapbox, extending my right foot forward, and his hands
went to work like they were an heir to brancusi, moving in
delicate circles, soothing the material's achings, the
accidental kick, the wear and tear of everyday weather,
the ramifications of daily living, running the smooth towel
across their geography like a jeweler, my shoes glittering in
the crisp autumnal light of the city, like they were beacons
protecting me from the grasping hands of the pickpocket's
hard luck story, the leer of the street kid demanding my
wallet, the gang cornering me into oblivion on a walk on
the wrong side after midnight, i was safe in the cocoon of
my shined shoes from any disturbance threatening to
rattle my timbers, moving lightly along broadway, like a
gentleman with an appointment with a success story,
when every surface of the city was turned by the lathe of
the immigrants' aspirations, making this city gleam under
the lamps of gas light, when the avenues were consumed
by the bustle of people moving through the tumult graced
with the casual elegance of satin, nylon hose, a hat tipped
in the appropriate direction.

THE MAN WITH THE MAGNIFYING GLASS

his magnifying glass inspected the finer shades of every atom, every echo, every reverberation. the dilapidated wall of a tenement on east 10th street, the graffiti sprayed by a gang of horny adolescents, the blood spilling from a self-inflicted wound. he'd pull his magnifying glass from his pocket in the grandstand of yankee stadium and observe the velocity of a 100 mile-an-hour fastball, the turning of a lingering curveball, the drop of a slider leaving the batter motionless as a statue. he'd spend saturday afternoons in the park analyzing the bark of a five-hundred-year-old maple, the crossing of pollen by bees in a hurry to fly home to the mother lode of honey. he'd pay visits to the museum of non-objective art in search of the meaning of abstraction, scratching his head in wonder at the streak of mustard yellow in a canvas by de kooning. he'd sit investigating a granual of sugar, the accidental shake of pepper, the foam rising from a cup of capucchino like a snow-capped mountain in the andes. he'd return home to his tiny apartment on a crime-riddled block near the east river, and climb the rickety stairs looking deeply through each keyhole in quest of learning the darkest secrets of his neighbors. then he'd quickly close each lock of his door, disappearing like nightfall, like the back side of the moon, like a rendezvous with death in a tragedy by shakespeare. his eyes zooming in like a camera, examining every cast shadow, every reflection, every gravestone.

WHERE DOES LOVE GO WHEN IT DIES?

where does love go when it dies? under a rock in a jealous
lover's garden? does love vanish in a shell's ear or float in
the nether reaches of interstellar space along with useless
satellites? when love dies does it fizzle like a flat glass of
seltzer or is it explosive as a rocket carrying armageddon
on its shoulders? when love dies can it be brought to life
by jesus' touch or the gypsy in the window round the
corner? does love die in a whimper suffocated by a pillow?
the quaking roar of a heart pummeled by the sturm and
drang of dissatisfaction pressing the peddle to the floor?
does love die because of a suddenly unappetizing smell?
a need to move on to something other? a flash of
enlightenment saying there's nothing here to hold on to
anymore? and when love dies does it get buried in a park
where couples picnic throwing springtime around like an
aphrodisiac? or does it humbly walk down a blind alley
crying softly to itself? maybe love doesn't die at all. maybe
love's merely awaiting a return to the senses. maybe love's
merely lurking under a hat or in a poem written on the
bathroom wall or on a tree's bark celebrating the intials of
our names wrapped round by a funny slightly lumpy
shaped heart.

WHEN THEY'RE INSIDE YOU
THEY HEAR

when they're inside you
they hear
every tug of a collar
every button snapping
every amen in holy communion
when they're inside you
they hear
the mouth drawing liquid from a cup
the circuitous route of a bowl of clam chowder
the reverberations of a lip
lingering on a nipple
when they're inside you
they hear
the wagging tail of a dog in the podiatrist's office
the brim of a hat shading the skin from rain
the television blabbing
about purchasing
physic redemption
on
credit
when they're inside you
they hear
the body's rising and falling in sleep
the throbbing inside the brain's muscle
the quick pulse of light under the eyelids
the words murmured
in the throes of a nightmare
questioning
the
symbolism
of a boat's
hurdle
over

the
crest
of
niagara
when they're inside you
they hear
the shootdown in a western
ending in a quick draw
ending in silence
ending in burial
on a windy prairie
when they're inside you
they hear
every argument climbing to denouement
the bolts of a lock yielding to numbers
the key slipping in the tumblers
the rumble of a train
off in the distance
when they're inside you
they hear the escape of water down a drain
the pitter pat of sweat soaking up a forehead
the emergency voice
over the radio
warning
of
a sixty second high shriek
preparing us for
the second coming of noah
when they're inside you
they hear
when they're inside you
they hear
when they're inside you
they hear
the
babbling

of
a
new
life
awaiting
entrance
naked
bloody
crying

THE LITTLE GIRL THREW BLACK PAINT ON HER MOMMY'S WEDDING DRESS

the little girl the little girl threw black paint threw black paint on her mommy's wedding dress on her mommy's white satin wedding dress because she didn't want to share her mommy with some guy who'd crack her over the head when he caught her setting her dolls on fire or plucking out their eyeballs or traveling their body with her tongue licking their plastic skin because it gave her a chill of pleasure and demanding they kiss her they undress her they climb her like a hill in the park like her real daddy used to do when her mommy was out shopping because he was a good daddy because he always bought her ice cream with sprinkles always called her his fragrant little garden then he'd stick her head in the oven to see how long she could hold her breath before coughing or order her to recite her times tables while he tied her tongue to the whirling ceiling fan so she launched a bucket of black paint of black paint on her mommy's wedding dress on her mommy's white satin wedding dress because she didn't want anyone getting under the covers asking for favors she wanted to play with her dolls alone to brush their long blond hair to rub cream over their smooth skin to make them soft make them melt make them ooh and aah because then nobody could take them away nobody could steal them nobody could interfere with the naughty lessons she taught them

THE POET OF DIVAS AND CANARIES
AND RENAISSANCES

for joseph cornell

he was the man of boxes, constructed of pine, nailed
together, and covered by a pane of glass, his life small
and intimate as images in an envelope, spilling, falling,
disappearing in the vortex of a tornado, ethereal as rain,
as air, as fog, because he was a poet of divas and
canaries and renaissances, his mind tipping toward the
dead rising and lifting a drink to heaven, like a child in a
poem by blake, singing in the elysian fields with lambs,
saving himself for god's private conversations in his ear,
whispering about the meeting of a rose with a schooner
on a piece of paper sailing into sky.

MR. CHING

written in collaboration with
Lenny DellaRocca

yesterday
while walking
in a mirrored room
at the amusement park
while
breathing
in
spring
time
while
reading
a poem by
e
e
cummings
about
love
in
inclement
weather
i was aroused
by
the
memories
of
the
small brown bowls
by mr. ching.
i remember walking
through the rooms
of the famous
ceramicist's house

in kyoto
observing the tinkle of rain
on the skylight
the running of a cat
across the red carpet
the song of a cardinal
in the flute of a musician
in the wet garden.
i was still young enough then
to believe in
zen/beauty/and good deeds.
now she has returned home
and braves the toothy storm
of late summer
swallowing everything up in dampness
and the heavy blankets of memory.
she paints a still life
of bones and coral and photographs
of herself reflected in mirrors
in the funhouse of her imagination
where buddha sits
laughing
and
throwing
peanuts.
someday i will rescue her
from her wanderings
but now i sleep
in this big soft chair
dreaming of
raking
stones
on

a
quiet
afternoon
in
cherry
blossom
season
along
the
river
zbu.

THE SPACE BETWEEN TREES

*"The space between trees is art enframed by
imagination."—16th century zen master*

the space between trees
something
left
behind
in
the memorable echo
of a high tenor
scaling the heights
of
don giovanni
or
the invincible air of a mountain
in a print by hiroshige
brushed
on
to
paper
by
a
wish
and
a
prayer
the space between trees
unmeasurable
by
the
unerring
eye
of
a
renaissance

master
discovering the amplitude
of
perspective
in
the distant light of christ's crucifixion
the space
between
trees
like
in
a
painting by de chirico
everything casting
an impossible shadow
over a still afternoon
the space between trees
like buddha explaining
the
unknowingness
of
all
things
to
a
small
child
holding
her arms open
in
a
spring
field
of
budding
trees

THE WOMAN WITH THE VIDEO CAMERA

THE WOMAN WHO LOVED THE BICYCLE HELMET

she loved his bicycle helmet, so when they broke up because he was too fragile to run his fingers across her pores, between the thighs of her conversation, inside the hollows of her breathing, she placed the helmet on her head and it wrapped around her like the scent of lilies on an april morning, her ears cupped by its cradle, like the interior of a shell, creating a pocket of air, whistling like the music of a wind chime, her head held in an ocean of hands, like waves lapping on a seashore, where every harsh word was forgiven, where trust was something held onto, where distance would not become them, as she lifted her body pirouetting onto the bicycle rotating her legs bending forward creating a vacuum between her mind and heart so she could race forward into the night

I THOUGHT I HEARD A KEY IN THE DOOR

i thought i heard a key in the door and you were coming
home again, the tumblers unlocking, your footsteps
reaching across the checker-board floor, your body slipping
under the bed sheets, perching close to my existence, you
did not try to convince me i was the improper lover for your
karma, your voice holding a conversation with the starlight,
your eyes facing beyond the periphery i offered, you were
not sand slipping through my fingers, a shadow vanishing
in a crack in the corner, you were coming home for the
consistency of my temperature, the comfort i provided
when you were wounded, for what you had mistaken for
anger, for resentment, for charity, i thought i heard a key
in the door and you were coming home again, writhing
in passion for the rhythm of my breathing

EVERY RUMOR YOU HEAR ABOUT ME
IS TRUE

every rumor you hear about me is true. i'm a gypsy moth
hibernating inside your sweater. i'm a spyglass pressed
against your eyelid. i'm a mirror for your imagination.
i feed your arousal. enticing you with lewd stories. feeding
the coal oven of your expectations. stirring up your desires
like a fly settling on your warm shoulder. i'm a vampire of
sexuality. behind that door i'm an animal, carnivorous.
a flesh eater. i don't leave any bones. i clean up everything
on my plate. actually i'm a void, a hole. something to step
down in. i'm empty. i'm frozen. i'm sexually inhibited.
i've got more problems than you can wave a cat at. every
conversation with you is a purr. a reach across my table.
a long distance kiss in the dark. but i'll only flirt with your
expectations. i'll make you simmer. i'll arouse you with
every rumor. then disappear out your doorstep.

THE ADVENTURES OF LASSIE

as a boy i was a regular member of the sunday evening american television audience tuned in to the adventures of lassie. my face pressed within smelling distance of the black and white screen serving up an imaginary scenario starring lassie the wonder dog and her perfectly mannered rural american family breaking bread together in a plain as nails farmhouse. i wanted to work out a trade with god and become golden-locked blue-eyed deep-dimpled little timmy always deferring to the house rules of his beautiful mommy and daddy, whose grainy voices never rose far above a whisper in some perfect heartland setting, a million starry miles from the reality of my brick lined neighborhood in brooklyn, where emotion smashed its fists on the dinner table. i wanted lassie as a bodyguard in my daily peregrinations with the reality of the school yard, to tackle the bully of the neighborhood, to save me from accidental slips into manholes, to shield me from the bickering conversation of my parents over the rising cost of my hand-me-down clothes. i wanted to climb inside the small rectangular screen and live with my big brainy dog, with the elegant thinness of katherine hepburn, the smooth as sugar glide of roger banister, accompanying my perilous walk beyond childhood's bruised knees, with the courage of a greek mythical hero daring medusa to eyeball em into stone.

PIRATE FENWICK

someday i'm going to discover
pirate fenwick's galleon
but till then
i'll dig
at the crest of high tide
with my shovel
searching for a souvenir of his conquests
because
pirate fenwick's
my hero
i've dedicated a scrapbook to his swagger
and memorized every one
of his swash buckling adventures
sometimes i put a patch over my eye
pretending i'm pirate fenwick
muttering curses from my seaworn mouth
till my mother tells me it's time for bed
and i dream all night about
swiss cheesing
a ship's crew and captain
with my bravado
cutting off their ears
and adding them to my collection
then sentencing them to a silent walk
off the gangplank
into shark infested waters
and when i wake up
all refreshed from another night of plunder
i head to the seashore with my shovel
digging and digging and digging
in quest of a gold nugget
robbed by

my hero
pirate fenwick
because
i won't give up
being persistent
till sunset closes the eyes of daylight
and my mother calls me home for supper

WHITE

e
v
e
r
y
t
h
i
n
g'
s
whiter
than a ku klux klansman's bed sheets
than a piece of chalk
screeching across the blackboard
than a bouquet of lilies
sticking out their stamens and pistils
to
the
ear
of
god
on easter sunday
whiter
than a painting
by
kasimer malevich
whiter
than an art gallery wall
sticking its tongue out
at whistler's nocturne
in pink and blue
whiter
than that line of cocaine

making my nose itch
whiter
than a ticker tape parade
in the canyon of heroes
whiter
than an anglo-saxon baby's butt
than that polar bear
who promised to keep me warm
during nuclear winter
than
those gloves worn by the rich lady
allergic to the poor sleeping in the alleyway
so rest your head upon a feather pillow
get under a fleece blanket
and sleep till you wake up
on a white xmas
on a morning so white
you have to wear sunglasses
or you'll be permanently blinded
then
w
h
I
t
e
out
this
poem
making a fresh start
on a brand new piece of paper
creating
a
perfectly counted haiku
crowding so much meaning
on
the

head
of
a
matchstick
struck against the sidewalk
summing up the universe
like a miscalculation
flying out of the orbit
of common thinking
or
the cosmic force
of a child's
perfectly
round
snowball

NO

on the marble table
she
left
small
almost microscopic
granules
of cocaine.
no.
she quickly covered herself with kerosene
and asked her ex-husband to ignite her.
no.
on the roof she ate a sandwich
before spreading her wings
like an eagle
and
jumping.
no.
everyone considered her a piece of a puzzle
lost in the great chicago fire.
no.
the car.
the road.
the infinite rope
of a trail
of
impossible
promises.
no.
the heart falling flat on its face
like an off kilter tennis shot.
no.
the racket in the kitchen.

no.
the assumption that fell on the doorstep.
no.
the kleptomaniac who lives with memories
of a stolen diamond necklace.
no.
the hairs growing from her eyeball like in a painting by
salvador dali.
no.
she's spinning out of the grasping fingertip reach
of a metaphor she's incapable of becoming
friendly
with.
no.
she's receding into the wall like an old woman in a
painting by edouard vuilliard.
no.
her existence vanishing behind a dark comeuppance.
no.
the sea stretching out its welcome
like coleridge in the rhyme of the ancient mariner.
no.
when she stepped out of the house
her skin glowed
like she was radioactive.
no.
the people on the street buckled
like they had recently returned
from a sojourn
at the madame curie clinic.
no.
he was rapidly approaching the woman
tied to the track.
no.
then after the sun had fallen into the sea

she slept like a storybook
in his arms
dreaming
of
springtime
and
honey.

MY MOMMA LEFT ME THESE PEARLS

my momma left me these pearls. sometimes when i hold
them up to the light i see her paddling little jimmy on the
behind or strumming on that old washboard and my vision
gets tangled in the underbrush. i just lay there even when
a breeze comes and licks my face. these pearls protect me
since she's gone. they roll across my fingers like momma's
hands telling me don't cry or i'll get my dress wrinkled,
and i listen to momma. even when i've been wandering for
days picking berries to feed my stomach. i've been walking
so long i don't know what county i'm in but the boys at the
seven-eleven always say soft things that smooth out my
clothes and lift them over my head. when they drive me
down the road i'm still holding these pearls in my hand.
shaking em like a hula hoop or unfurling em when the
beads get knotty. i keep them sparkling like a sky full of
stars. like when you look up and you don't know where the
tail on the universe is there's so much whiteness out there
twinkling and curving like a chalk line on a blackboard.
i rub and rub till my fingers get worn and i start shaking
like i'm being turned inside a wash tub and i hold on tight
to these pearls till my body's quieted down cause my
momma'd spank me for not taking good care of what she
left when she passed on. i've got to keep walking now so
i can find my way home before winter comes, and put
fresh flowers down by my momma's headstone.

THE JUNK MAN DOWN THE HILL

that'll cost you thirty cents. be careful with that thing or it'll backflip you in the eye. happened to me after my sons took off. rebuking me for wanting them to become part of the family junk business. they had other prettier sights in mind. i never counted on that happening. when they was kids they'd scoot around here piling things and adhesing the broken wing on anything. one time mrs. mcgillicuty brought over her ailing lawnmower and they propped it up and got it to sing more beautiful than that pop star frankie avalon. i mostly mind my business here. don't have the right to be messing in anybody's stew but my own. jimmy petrie and the boys working the rig in clementown ain't gonna succeed in hypnotizing me to come out and get drunk. did that. don't do that no more. go to church now. praise the lord. that's seventy five cents. aw, take it for fifty. my wife and i are regular missionaries. helping with communions. dunking the kids or handing them a holy wafer. you can have that for a nickle. my boys say i'm pound-foolish. cause they take after the way their dad once wuz with the booze and the ladies and the loudness storming around with a big shoe and stepping it down on any pesky thing that moves. sick of them flies. sick of them mosquitoes. sick of them sons of mine for leaving me blind like that. i'm planning to build another shed over there. and a deck for the mrs. and a swimming pool for my grandkids if they show up someday and make me feel proud. that ain't no good. go on and take it for free. maybe i will pull a tall one on tonight. six years without a drink so maybe i deserve some. stlll got a gallon of the homemade hooch in the storm cellar wrapped up in muslin and cotton towels. i'll raise a drink to my missing boys and the junk overflowing so i can't ever keep track of what i own. that'll be a dollar and a half and six cents for that. put it all together and you can have it for a dollar.

SOMETIMES WILLY COOS UP
TO RHYME

sometimes willy coos up to rhyme. leaning on it like a
lover. brushing its hair. pinching its behind. caressing
rhyme. tongue kissing rhyme. running his hands over
rhyme's body. and sometimes willy insists we justify
the closure of our sentences with an a b a b rhyme
scheme. that god meant us to speak in quatrains.
that the world's gone downhill since the elizabethan age.
that free verse has gotten us in deep doo doo. maybe
crazy willy has something. maybe i better start speaking in
sonnets or villanelles. maybe i better mind the way i end
lines — justifying their conclusions with more appropriate
framing — a more musical way of surrendering to the
unfathomability of language. its porousness. its holy
surrender to weak words that leave their stain on our skin
or clothing. their modern bareness incapable of giving in
to romance or beauty or passionate sweet nothings.
next time i see willy i'm going to join him in a long thick
parade of rhymes setting the universe upright.

THE MAN OF ABBREVIATIONS

he abbreviated the world, whittling it with his language,
paring it down like a botanist examing the heart of
a flower, his ear pressed against its petals, listening to
the whir of pollen, reducing everything to its latin
derivation, like darwin proscribing the ranking of every
insect, bird, and human; and then he'd sleep, dreaming of
becoming a reed waving in the wind, a drop of water
falling from the moist petal of a rose, a stone in a quarry
awaiting the arrival of a mason; because he was drifting
out to sea like mercury or quicksilver, a raft drifting along
the turns of the louisiana bayou and stripping the world of
everything that veers from our senses, like a runaway train
killing forty; breaking the world down to something pure,
lean, accountable, so he could sit with the objects of his
mission, convincing every harsh word to turn into a
whisper; then he'd vanish along the path down to the river,
covering himself with fallen branches, rubbing soil into
the pores of his skin, and abbreviating the world into a
small box he could hide in.

THE WOMAN WITH THE VIDEO CAMERA

she videotaped the way rain fell in hard diagonals/the white noise emanating from the grayness of the tv screen/how the atmosphere affected personality disorders/how the weather shaped the destinies of muslims/the bouncing of children on beds while the babysitter was sleeping/the arrangement of mirrors of tables of lamps of pictures on walls/how light coated every face/how hair grows on a head/she videotaped the textures of surrender/the cool breath of a stranger on a neck/the hand's passage up a thigh/the soft pressing of fingers on a groin/she aimed her camera at the runners jogging/the dinner parties foiled by a burnt chicken/the drunken antics of an uncle puffing cigar smoke/the geometry of windows maintaining their rigid attitude against the dirt/she turned the camera on the reunion of mothers and daughters/the warm creasing embrace/the kisses upon cheekbones/the visitations of grandchildren on xmas/the streamers extending out of mouths on new year/the traffic inside whore houses/the movement of men entering rooms removing hats removing gloves removing scarfs removing topcoats removing pants removing undergarments/she videotaped every nuance of color/every pore marking survival/every grip on the banister/every foot rising up/every shoe being tied/her eyes absorbing the protocol of nightlight saying come undress me with your camera penetrate every dominion

YOUR HANDS ARE THE SUBJECT
OF THIS POEM

your hands are the subject of this poem. and i reach for
them across a barbwire fence, across a foxhole, across a
millennium of humiliation, awaiting the bull's-eye of a
bullet. your hands are the noun. verb. adjective. and be all.
even when they're cold, ornery, combative. your hands
slapping me when i'm silly. rendering me an example.
pointing me out in the schoolyard. your hands collaring me
when i play hooky from responsibilities. running from our
kids. ignoring them when they ask questions about my
disappearances from the dinner table. your hands tapping
me on the shoulder. asking for solace. asking for loving. but
i run from those hands. because they corner me. they ask
me to own up to my sins. i veer from any demonstrations of
affection. i take comfort in church on sunday. on my knees
before the altar. before the statue of the holy mother.
before the priest pressing closer to hear my confession.
like a car skidding away from a hit and run accident.
avoiding owning up to the persecution of your hands.
your beautiful hands. your beautiful beautiful hands.

EVERY WALL HAS A STORY TO TELL

every wall has a story to tell. these walls are thin to any conversation. pressing up against them i can witness venice in thomas mann's time — the cupid shooting an arrow — the discretion of a turn of the century era — before cubism became passé and duchamp was still a toddler in short pants. as i said every wall's a good conversationalist. every wall deserves a backrub. every wall loves an occasional paint job or the plugging of its holes. these walls are culpable. these walls are guilty. these walls are ashamed. they are easily bruised by marbles, windows, posters of women wearing more make-up than clothing. these walls stick their tongues out. these walls are naughty. sometimes i sit staring at their pock-marked surface. imagining india, bejing, constantinople. these walls enclose muslims in prayer. incense rising. the odor of camels. bedouins smoking from a hookah. these walls remind me of the sanctuary in florence where fra angelico painted angels till he was blinded by their light. these walls point me off on a mission. tie my shoes. tighten my tie. shoo me off like i'm about to begin a long adventure as an apprentice to a magician — becoming adept at pulling rabbits from air or cutting blond tressed damsels into thirds. these walls surround me with their baaing, their mooing, their yodeling. and when i close my eyes i'm mountain climbing in grundenwald and there's no wall i won't stretch my frame over. sit with this wall. pet it. caress it. adore it. say "good wall." invite it in for the night.

MICKEY MANTLE

i
remember
your
country
boy
good
looks
your
neck
broad
as
oklahoma
your
skin
fair
as
midwestern
reserve
your
body
looking
like
it
was
packed
with
alfalfa
like you'd been bred
to
strike
a
baseball
a

country
mile
you
were
the
last
american
hero
before
oswald
shot
down
camelot
before
the
napalmed
sky
crashed
down
on
american
innocence
before
the
media
went
on
a
lynching
party
blackening
the
eye
of
every
hero

the
country
boy
biting
into
the
golden
apple
your
knees
scarred
up
from
chasing
everything
hit
to
deep
center
circling
the monuments
to
the
iron
horse
and
the
babe
while
hodgkins
disease
followed
your
family
line

hoping
to
catch
up
to
you
by
forty
as you waited for your pitch
slugging the tar out of it
to
win
at
the
ballpark
up
on
161st
street
alleviating
the
city
of
its
unlucky
burdens
r.
i.
p.
big
guy

FLAVOR

i remember your taste
the way you flitted on my tongue
the aroma of everything you bit
the music you made when you spun
around my forefinger
the writhing in the sack
in the middle of the
night
catching you from
falling
the way morning
lifted your eyebrows
afternoon made you pronounce your vowels
evening sweltered on your fingertips
i want to hold what i can remember
so tight my hands tremble
the flavor of you
seeping into my skin's pores
like a strong drink
at the end of a terrible day
but it's too late for that
unfortunately
you're dead
just a fragrance
on a handkerchief
i forgot to wash
some smell sucked
in my nostrils
in an earlier life
that causes me to itch
my skin allergic
to your chemical composition
and that's all burnt up
the ashes in your urn

on top of my piano
just a shadow
of the lover
i remember
filling my day to day life
with terrible temper tantrums
with trouble
with tragedy
with a lot of things
beginning with t
no you do not rest upon my baby grand
no you are not a victim of death's long reach
no you are not someone i still send postcards to in brooklyn
your flavor
has slipped off
my tongue
and i can
no longer find it
no longer hulk against it when i'm cold
no longer use it as evidence that i'm alive
no longer be a witness to its miracle

THIS MORNING I WAS PLANNING TO WRITE A POEM

this morning i was planning to write a poem about getting old, without any family, friends, neighbors or social workers looking on, when the breathing's labored, when legs and arms turn rubbery, when the eyelids get heavy as a ton of sand holding back a tidal wave, and the world's a thin blurry strip of locomotion and light, and it doesn't help moaning thirty years too late about not raising a family so someone could read you the daily comics, so you could continue to keep in touch with the peregrinations of nancy and sluggo, but then i started thinking of writing a poem about the impact of crack on the motor coordination of subway conductors, the rising percentage of junior high school girls lifting their skirts for a quarter, the number of city buildings living on a decline, the resourcefulness of released mental patients learning to hum the sound track of the film *it's a wonderful life* while raising coins with a fishing line and hook through a metal grating, but by then i was feeling sorry for myself and wanted to write a poem about the total weight of the drugs i devoured in high school while doing my homework, but autobiographical poems bore me and i thought again of writing a poem about the two guys who've been living outside my apartment window wrapped in makeshift blankets made out of the *times, post* and *daily news*, and about how they're wrapped in an enormous quantity of words helping them sleep on the cement, but then i abandoned that idea too, and decided it wasn't a good morning to write a poem after all.

POETIC JUSTICE

THE AUTOMATS OF THE CITY

as a child i was mesmerized by the automats of the city —
the polished gleam of black and silver art deco cupboards
bearing treasures in even rows behind plate glass doors.
i'd throw in nickels gathered from the ever-present apron of
the cashier and wait with baited breath for the unlatching of
my dreams, scanning the high ceilinged room as vast to my
young eyes as an iowa wheat field, where citizens of the city
gathered at circular tables communing on the conversation
of the day; shaking heads at the tempestuous turning of the
weather, the embattled warlords of city hall shuffling money
from pockets to seams in the mattress, the sounds leaping
from saxophones on west fifty second street, the saturday
evening post surrealism of dwight and mamie's reign in the
white house, cleanly drawn and painted by norman rockwell,
ruffles smoothed of every uncompromising wrinkle, in
defense against russians snapping top secret blueprints with
cameras hidden in the baby-blue diamond pattern in a silk
dress tie. these were the meeting halls of post-world war II
urban america, after the rise of the unions and the advent of
the minimum wage and the rock, chisel, brush, and pencil of
the wpa and buddies asking can you spare a dime. it was the
coming age of coca-cola and the beat generation and the
grinding pelvis of early rock and roll and thalidomide. but in
the womb of the gleaming art deco cafeterias i felt safe from
nuclear submarines threatening to tangle the fishing lines of
the harbor, leatherjacketed gangs switchblading each other
over enemy turf in brooklyn, and the french putting their
dukes up across the dmz line. my stomach warmed over easy
by an open roast beef sandwich, mashed potatoes, green
beans, and the soapbox talk of immigrants whose rough
hewn hands laid down the bricks of this city in anticipation of
a glorious microwave future for their children.

THE LITTLE GIRL AND THE BEAN PLANT

the little girl nestled a bean plant in the crack in the pavement praying to mother mary that it would be fortified by the dirt of the city that it would stand tall against any footfalls jarring interruption or heavy wind blowing its cheeks out at its branches like the bully of the block pulling her hair and running. the little girl returned daily with a pail of water quenching the plant's struggles to grow green. and the bean plant was resilient as a child learning the ropes of the ghetto meandering through the battlefield in front of the schoolyard pretending to be nothing more than a shadow on the sidewalk and grew taller than any fable in a book of pictures fighting off slingshots. and the little girl climbed the bean plant one summer afternoon till she sat on its crown waving at passing airplanes at clouds at angels and the little girl climbed down snapping off beans as she traveled and passed them into the arms of the city to the butcher to the baker to her mother and father to the firemen awaiting her with a ladder to the cool kids who had always shaken her off like a flea. and the neighborhood feasted on the greenness that she had grown with her small hands like a miracle burning bright in a myth making believers of even the muttering old women and men who shuffled across the sidewalk with a plague on all houses replenishing hope like a wishing well like a prayer like a phoenix rising from the ashes.

MY FAMILY BURIAL GROUND IS SINKING INTO THE EARTH

my family burial ground is sinking into the earth.
before winter passes the earth will capture every stone.
the earliest arrival was great grandpa purlis who spent his
kindling years in pocomoke city gathering strength for the
hard climb to these parts to turn the soil every season for
old man mccarthy. the final arrival on this plot was cousin
wilmetta who died like a withered branch of tuberculosis
in the winter of '36. there's the marker of captain hudson
who my great aunt sarah cared for at the end of his long
respectful life in the shipping line. someday no one will
know this ground was a mourning field greeting the
hereafter. the small poem on each grave keeping their
spirits alive will be swallowed for eternity into the soil.
the grass will cover my heritage and corn will be planted
and rise high over their heads.

MY SISTER MAGDELENA WAS ENGAGED TO BE MARRIED TO GUISEPPE

my sister magdelana was engaged to be married to
guiseppe, who learned a trade at the industrial school on
st. mark's place and promised to carry her away from the
long days of toil sewing for pennies from her padrone,
and the fire started like a whisper, hesitantly, like it was
pausing in a corner before it looked into the face of god,
then it caught on a waistband, and a moan rose from
each floor, and the fire traveled like it was burning through
paper, because pounds of fabric burn easily, creating a
cauldron of screams and rips and tears, searing through
skin like it was made of cotton, like it was flimsy, and one
narrow window led to a staircase that fell under the weight
of panic, and the elevator cables snapped when someone
slid down them, and the firemen's ladder reached only the
sixth floor, many died without moving, their skin seared to
the bone, and some sat at the window's edge kissing the
star of david or crossing themselves and saying a prayer to
jesus to save them before jumping to the pavement, and
magdelena was caught in the backlash of a curl of fire,
closing her mouth with one finger, instructing her to be
quiet, to lay down, till she was ashen, till she floated
through the charred air of lower broadway, drifting toward
the east river, like a black cloud in the late winter sky.

RIKER MOUNTAIN

this house is made of hewn timber. the shingles hand split
by my great grandfather timothy riker when he wasn't
much more than a boy. this is the only house still standing
— it's a witness to when this mountain's soil was fertile
and you could spit and it would grow into something
worthwhile. sometimes i open my great grandfather's diary
and read about bert dalley, who moved here following his
release from libby prison after the civil war — sometimes
you'd hear him howl in the middle of the night, and pull out
his shotgun, shooting at tin cans and naming them after
confederate generals, till they took him away for trying to
round up a posse to catch john wilkes booth whom he said
he heard down in the creek bellowing shakespeare in a
southern drawl, or willy crossey who bought his land sight
unseen in 1911 and couldn't ever squeeze out a living
from the by now wrung-out-earth, who died a poor man
homesick for the ireland sod, cremated by his widow sarah
who buried his ashes in the wall surrounding their house,
marking his spot with a ring of small stones. there were
once more than seventy trees lining this road, and stately
old maples still line where i'm standing. most of the folks
who lived here are buried in that upper cemetery, even
those who went away and requested they be brought back
home. some of the graves are unmarked and others are
carved carefully in marble, surrounded by white cedars,
arbor vitae, the tree of life, keeping on the spirits of the
long dead, and those who sold out their farms in the years
since 1921 when the hard rains swept through this town,
knocking down foundation walls, ripping apart cellarholes
and wells, shaking the lives of the families who made this
mountain grow till the fertility ran out on the steep, clear
slopes and the flatter, richer and freer western lands lured
them on, but me and my family are moving back to riker

mountain. we're shooing away those things that just crowd up our lives and don't leave anything worthwhile in its tail. we're gonna raise the rafters of that old barn. we're gonna line up every fallen stone. we're gonna write our names in metal in a broad arch. we're claiming what's ours and what never should have been lost.

A JOURNAL OF EACH DAY

a
journal
of
each day.
each season.
each echo.
the reverberation of elms falling in a forest.
the cantata by bach rimming the stone walls
of the cathedral.
the fisherman's line
yielding to speckled trout
on a river in new england.
the voice over the loudspeaker
at the minor league ballpark
informing us of a race
between a turtle
and a newborn child.
a
journal
recording
every twig.
every tree branch.
every family of oaks
nodding in the heat
of
midsummer.
the chipmunk scurrying across boulders
that have lain there
since the presidential election
of john quincy adams.
the voice of a young girl
combing her hair in the mirror
beside an open window.
a
journal

of
numbers.
equations.
a palm lowered in the sack of rice.
a pair of chopsticks.
a shovel.
a hoe.
ears pressing upon the journal's pages.
listening
for
chirps.
rivets.
cooing.
trains making their way along the earth's skin
like soldiers carrying fallen brothers home.
the landscape
trembling
in
anticipation
of
rain.
the majorette's baton
twirling in the air
like a mobile
choreographed
by
alexander calder.
a
journal
of
deliverance.
patience.
prayer.
a journal weary.
closing its pages.
folding up for the night.

IN A PERFECT WORLD

in a perfect world
this poem
would
be
a best seller
memorized by millions
grafittied on bar stools
evidence in court
able to disarm
the loudmouth
&
the querulous.
in a perfect world
this poem
would
heal the unhealthy
implicate the unworthy
clarify the subjunctive
should
could
or
must
be.
in a perfect world
i
would
never
make love with you
in a bomb shelter
i would write poems for you
like a striptease
nirvana would be an herb
eternal peace would be a cure
victories would be decided

with chicken bones.
in a perfect world
you & i
would
be
on the same side
of the rope
pulling the ideal
in a tug of war
with destiny.
in a perfect world
poems would be barter
and
i'd trade you lines
for
freedom.

I WAS DELIVERED BY WILLIAM CARLOS WILLIAMS

when i was plucked from the womb by william carlos
williams a haiku wailed out of my mouth and dr. williams
patted my rump and whispered in my ear that he liked my
poem because it was as tangible as the yowling of boys
sticking their feet in an icy river. and when i learned to
crawl dr. williams came to my playroom and pretended to
be a red wheelbarrow i'd cart around into imaginary
corners and together we'd investigate the dualities
clinging to rocks or bricks or pick-up-sticks or dandelion
seeds and lift our index finger to write wet words upon
frosted windows. dr. williams told me to open my eyes
big to everything passing within the radius of my
circumference like an ant carrying a crumb on her back
like a day laborer pungent with the odor of a rickety old
building like a woman seated motionless on a bed in a
painting by edward hopper. dr. williams was my childhood
companion on travels to abstract places outdistancing
narratives tumbling down the stairs and we'd hold a
telescope to our eye to witness atoms dancing in their
shells or waves cresting on a seashore. dr. williams
helped me understand the life force inside things
accidentally spilling or propped up so they stand tall or
dark as an eclipse of the sun and moon making us
scratch our head for the answers to all things intangible.
yes dr. williams delivered me to the world. bloody. crying.
grasping to understand the properties of steam. the
porousness of clouds. the elemental structure of the
air floating between us.

GRANDMOTHER MOVES HER TINY
SHRIVELED FINGERS

grandmother moves her tiny shriveled fingers along the
split ends of my hair. her face is wet like morning dew.
the poor thing tells me she will be dead before my next
birthday. but my uncle jimmy says she will outlive the kids
in the backyard alley teaching themselves to wire walk.
she asks me why the mother of three is skipping rope in
the courtyard. why the man on the street honks in a big
purple handkerchief. why the girl on the rooftop is covered
with the blood of chickens. why i want to hide in the closet
and try on my sister's clothes. my skin breaks out in hives
the size of walnuts. i crush each shell with a poem and
sleep pressed against my grandmother — holding onto her
breath like a child wary of death's appointment — shaking
her when she begins to dream — so she won't ever leave
me alone.

MY GRANDFATHER BELIEVED THE MOON
HAS THE FACE OF GOD

my grandfather believed the moon has the face of god,
craggy and beaten up by comets, and when i was a kid i'd
sit for hours while he told me stories about how the moon
was once like the garden of eden, the moon was golden,
the moon was perfect, and i'd listen to him talk about the
gyration of the moon's orbit, the dark side facing away,
disappearing into something exotic, something forbidden,
or how the moon's craters sometimes sparkle in the
sunlight like a fire's stoking their surface, how no matter
where we are in the earth's rotation we're spinning in the
same place somehow, witnessing the same crescent
moon in the sky, and i stared into his face like it was
the old moon, studying the way light played along his
eyebrows, illuminating his face, casting shadows across
his wrinkles, right there, right up there, the moon,
the good old moon, the moon.

AT AUDEN'S APARTMENT ON
ST. MARK'S PLACE

i remember the night i went up to auden's apartment for a
shot of whiskey and a poem. w.h. was practicing archery
— believing it improved the aim and flavor of each
rhyme/each rhythm. and sometimes auden covered his
face with a silk veil or trembled informing me of his fear
of every unknown word marking the future. his teeth
clattering like dirty dishes. later i fell asleep in a room the
dimensions of a cupola in one of auden's italian sonnets.
my eyes staring at a wall of small triangular holes
silhouetted against a brilliant light. on the other side i
heard a voice that resembled a choir in a requiem. again.
again. again. like a wave breaking on a seashore. like a
pendulum swinging. incessant. cryptic. the voice was like
a message loaded in a bottle and vaulted out to sea or a
giant puzzle that takes a century to decipher. and i was on
the other side of the wall breathing it in like a fish looking
for a body of H_2O to welcome me home. through a pair
of binoculars i saw it become a blur. a brushstroke in
a painting by de kooning. an answer to an unfathomable
question posed by a zen buddhist on st. mark's place. and
suddenly auden jumped into the night air like a firecracker,
or a tale of chinese goldfish swallowing each other's tails,
till there was no proof they had ever existed.

WHERE ARE ALL THE MISSING SOCKS
IN THE WORLD?

where are all the missing socks in the world? have they
run away from home in search of utopia? are they circling
the planet like an independent satellite configuring a way
to save the environment? is it possible to locate their exact
longitude and latitude with a global telescope or must we
hire a private detective to scope out the hidden by-ways,
rivers, underground tunnels, narrow passageways where
the lost socks are hiding? are they huddled together there
in deep conversation about bunions, overgrown toenails,
corns and other day to day fables about the poor life of
feet? or are they sunning themselves under the sway of a
casual life in the carribean slurping funny colored drinks
certain to jettison the mind of any grasp of reality? are
they sitting in a cafe in prague wiping away the tears of
another failed revolution or are they being transformed
into the hand puppets of make-shift children in
orphanages on the other side of the dmz line? is there
any possibility they'll reappear suddenly in our chest of
drawers matched up with their grieving mates like
midshipmen returning home from a long stay at sea or are
they damned to live apart from their loved ones drifting in
the miasma of lonesome singularity among the bottom
feeders of human existence unable to ever turn on the
light switch of a long-term relationship? yes where are all
the missing socks in the world that have left us
heartbroken, sobbing mournfully over the trials and
tribulations of 100 percent cotton, or wool, or a mix of
synthetic fibers in dynamic patterns recalling kandinsky's
bauhaus years, or the tinged subtleties of corot's rural
peasantry, or the rub-your-eyes-aliveness of a warhol wall

of mooing cows? yes lord please point us in the direction
of all the missing socks in the world and we'll gather them
up in our arms like santa, pulling them onto our shivering
toes, praying for some warmth and comfort, under the raw
weight of top-heavy leather shoes.

I POSED FOR JAKE POLLOCK IN
THE LATE 1940S

jake pollock? i posed for him in the late 1940's. you didn't
know he worked with models even during his abstract
expressionist years? jake always wore his collar up
around his face like he was hiding something. he was
embarrassed by his childhood in wyoming. he used to
brand his sister and then cut himself with a bowie knife.
he always was sweet to me and when we made love it
was like he was peeling back my skin and entering a part
of me where no one had ever been before. we'd clink
glasses and he'd fuck me and then i'd lay there naked
and he'd get inspired and start dripping paint. creating
canvasses full of human skulls and explosions of black
and red and green. i guess he never would have been the
painter he was if i hadn't stirred up his wildness. i guess
i was kind of responsible for him doing what he did. his
wife lee knew it was me who stirred him up. we once had a
fight at the cedar tavern in front of kline and de kooning.
slamming away at each other till jake butted in and
stopped it. jake was coming to see me the night he drove
off the highway. i was posing for picasso. we were sleeping
together and he wouldn't let me out of his sight. so i called
jake and told him i couldn't be with him anymore. anyway
i was with pablo that night jake went off the road. and
sometimes i remember when jake and i'd sit at a booth
at the cedar tavern and he'd stick his tongue in my mouth
darting it around and he'd get excited like when he was
spilling cans of color across the surface of his pictures
creating surprises that jumped out of his subconscious like
snakes or goblins or owls. yeah i love his paintings. they're
messy but transcendent. they leap and spit and sizzle.

SOMEDAY WHEN THE TREES WILL BECOME KINGS AGAIN

—for joanne

old man raymond
commanded
the
trees
to
fall
like pick-up-stix
and
darkness
descended
on
every
flower
fern
and
grassy meadow
in
the
camps
men clinked glasses
celebrating mother nature
on the run
but
i'm going to live to be a hundred
so i can come see
how big the trees have grown
i'll study
every leaf
every patch of moss
every wildflower
every bird call
listening

to
the wind's song in the treetops
the buzzing of bees in the clearing
the soft falling of water along the stream beds
i will drink from
every spring
every pond
every river
yes
someday
when the trees
will become kings again

I WRITE ACROSS CANVASES

i write across canvases because then everyone can know
what i'm thinking when i'm painting. this canvas requires an
underground of red because i'm in a deep mood. resonant.
gleaming. like a samovar from turn-of-last-century russia
shined daily by a devoted peasant. on the surface
i make marks with my brush creating a whirlpool of action
that scares away flies and ticks and mosquitoes attracted
by its stickiness. this turbulence leads me on like a wayfarer
on a pilgrimage to mecca. and i turn toward the night sky
seeking a constellation that will show me the way home. the
canvas is now covered with stars of david and crosses and
twinkling dots on a black field. i brush away the symbols of
religion and look deeply into my canvas in search of the
origins of the universe. yes that's what this canvas is about.
the origins of the universe. how impressive. how profound.

I'M LIVING IN MY CAR

i've known cars since i was knee high to a grasshopper. my daddy used to rebuild em for fun in our yard. lots of old junked up cars that seen better days you could see stretching around in the weeds and down in the gulch. people would just drop them off like he was some kind of automobile undertaker and we'd scavenge through the wrecks of people's lives finding chipped teeth and rotting blood stains and broken bones and once we found part of a human skull with the hair still half hanging out and my little brother billy brought out his electronic microscope and we saw maggots running like they were in training for the olympics. these tattoos you're looking at tell the full unexpurgated story of my life. that's me at fourteen stealing from the rich people on henry street and getting put away in forbes reformatory until i could fend for myself at seventeen. this tatoo's got my dreamed for filling station with endless free air for the kids on bicycles. this tattoo? that's the grim reaper. he's already come and taken my brothers phil and denny the night their pickup turned circles like a roller coaster on millhouse road. this tatoo's my fantasy girl — blond — blue eyed — pert — big breasted. this is the tattoo i told you about. the one which took eight straight hours to put on with my tatooer melvin talking continuously about cars and guns and hunting beaver in canyon creek soon as the first day of autumn comes. by the way your car's running fine now. just keep an eye out to see it don't leak after the last drips of this oil can hit the road.

POETIC JUSTICE

is there such a thing as poetic justice? does it live
in my neighborhood or further uptown? does it
wear judicial robes and deliver solomonic decisions
in iambic pentameter? does it tip its hat to the
ghosts of ginsberg, bukowski and micheline? does
poetic justice roll up its sleeves helping at the
homeless shelter? is it fit and well-trimmed as a
haiku by basho? is it amused by the whitney
biennial? is it colorless? is it odorless? does it side
with mother nature against the mountain jack's
axe clearing our national forest? does poetic
justice prefer rap music, folk music or a broadway
musical picturing life as a song and dance routine?
does poetic justice carry a vowel upon its shoulder
differentiating what's masculine, feminine,
neutered or ambidextrous? let's sit down at the
bargaining table with poetic justice, arm wrestle
with poetic justice, break bread with poetic justice,
raise a toast to poetic justice.

ILLUMINATIONS

paintings by
Arturo Rodríguez

Arturo Rodríguez
Ghost Archipelago 1, 1999
Oil on canvas
52 x 68 inches

GHOST ARCHIPELAGO NO. 1

the door through your eye is open
a kite enters
becoming a leg
walking across the floors of your history
like
a
santa
ana
wind
sweeping the dust that has settled
from many years of struggle
across the pale landscape
of
bridges
homes
and
planes
becoming birds crashing into the earth
like bludgeoned sharks
the world
suddenly inhabited
by naked men fishing for secrets
in
your
remarkable
eyes
where
the darkest kind of disturbance lay
awaiting
a
spark
from
the pen of dante
these ghosts of the night

chaperoned
by
a
woman
holding
on
to
the
tail
of
a
blade
or
saxophone
or
paper
lamp
spilled
into
the
mouth
of
a
dream
where arms become the wings of ferocious
airplanes
spitting sulfur and bullets
and
a
woman's
head
is
devoured
by
questions pressed to her lips like prayers
on this archipelago

she
waits
for
a
hymn
to
circle
her
like
a
lasso
the hand of god on her shoulder
acknowledging
the
despair
of
a
run
of
eighth
notes
into
the
most
disturbing
currents
of
the
day
where
you
tip
your
hat
to
the

dead
an
exceptionally
polite
crow
making
a
tree
house
in
the
most
soulful
kind
of
oblivion
waiting
for
morning
to
drop
into
a
bucket
of
sun
light

ILLUMINATIONS

1

i come in
ready for swimming
or for the uncertainty
of your smile
across the barbwire of your chest
a whisper
comes
promising me
the certainty of your kiss
but there's too much thunder in this neighborhood
for any kind of erotic spill
instead
we observe the kid in the corner
wearing the spoked hat
hungering for the liberty of your arousal
the bells you ring
on
independence day
from any school of hard knocks
sometimes
we observe
the man at the dock
who knows the difference
between infinity and nothingness
like buddha opening his arms to bliss
out
there
a
lighthouse
burns
for every man's sins

Arturo Rodríguez
Illuminations 1, 2001
Oil on canvas
86 x 86 inches

and
a fisherman contemplates catching
the mother load of fish
in this unpremeditated room
the clouds
pass
without
requiring
any
labor
everything twists sideways
in the shape of a diamond
he climbs and climbs and climbs

2

come
i'll help you up the ladder
extend your hand
and i'll grab you
from your dreams
serenading you with my trumpet
the tunes you remember as a child
the tunes that lifted you
from the hard ground of the world
the tunes that inspired you to look closely
at mother nature's patterns
over there the mountains spill their beauty out
like droplets into the sea
over there the sky turns emerald blue
surrendering to beauty
for beauty's sake
over there i grab you
carefully
tenderly
so you can witness
what it is like

to be free
there the child with the paper crown
will nod his head yes
there the plants will grow as large as the moon
and you will try the day on
like a new shirt
covering your tender skin
from the implications
of the sun
hurdling its bright hands
across the dark memories
of
a
crosser
day
when the sky tumbled down
like a rock slide
and you ran
into the emptiness
of my arms
and I pressed you up
against
the
day
holding you there
measuring out your pain
with my long fingers
and carried you off
on my shoulders
over the mountains
like a divine vision
of
what
tomorrow
will
bring

Arturo Rodríguez
Iluminations 2, 2002
Oil on canvas
86 x 86 inches

Arturo Rodríguez
Illuminations 3, 2002
Oil on canvas
86 x 86 inches

3

your teeth
occupy my hand
it's a funny set of teeth
so funny it pushes me off the bed into oblivion
but i like oblivion
it catches me like a beachball
it swallows everything important whole
without spitting out the bones
yes
your teeth
occupy my hand
snapping shut
against my will
betraying
my loyalty
my faith
my meanness
when
i
was
only
joking
about
your punishment
your fate
your prison sentence
yes
your teeth
occupy my hand
while
staircases take my imagination
on the road
where children wearing sailboats on their heads
drag wonderment in from the world

where windows let in the light of redemption
where we run and run and run
from the pressing of your jaw
against the bones of
my
resurrection
the hard climb up from
the rock and roll bedrock of
our
world
throwing
poison
kisses
at
the
moon

4

your skin
talks to me of eve
and
the garden of innocence
where all doors close
to
indifference
here a woman bends
to
close
out
the
day
casting off dispersions
that tickle her despair
the door is pressed open
by one of nature's miracle workers

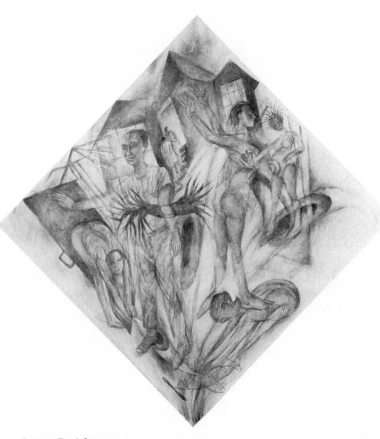

Arturo Rodríguez
Illumintions 4, 2002
Oil on canvas
86 x 86 inches

Arturo Rodríguez
Illuminations 5, 2002
Oil on canvas
86 x 86 inches

whose eyes are always blue
there is purity to these actions
a pushing aside of stale air
an unyielding of curtains
letting in the light
unhesitant
as a run of notes
across
the
piano's
keys
or
the certainty of the wind
on a blustery day
we imagine ourselves balanced
on the wings of an airplane
each corner of our world
open
to
a current of possibilities
or
the reaching of a hand to offer
an
apple
shaped
heart

5

we escape through a hole in the world
where a typhoon greets us with a nod
and
day welcomes us with
a glass of pernod
into the fray of our devotions

to the hobbyhorse of our childhood
and
the mistletoe of missed opportunities
we cough a thousand bullets like an angry gun
or
disassociate
becoming the train of a wedding dress
the brittle teeth of a petrified child
the floating magician looking for the keyhole
into the netherland of the dead
on the border
the guards are always awake
to the whir of an escaping boat
or
the turning of a bike's wheels
everything wrapped in a mummy's endless sheet
your portrait painted in wax and tears
atop a clown's endless skin
fearful of the hammering of the doctor's hands
and the sudden knock of the man who always has to be
on time
the light of the day
fierce
resilient
blue
a
smoky
blue
a
fathomless
blue

BRUCE WEBER grew up in the East Flatbush section of Brooklyn. He wrote his first poem at the age of eight, and became serious about writing while attending Far Rockaway High School. After completing course work for a Ph.D. in Art History at the City University Graduate Center, he moved to Washington, D.C., Kentucky and Florida, where he was active as an art historian, poet, poetry organizer and publisher. After working as a curator at the University of Kentucky Art Museum, the Norton Museum of Art and the Sackner Archives of Concrete and Visual Poetry, Weber returned to New York in 1990 and took a position as Director of Research and Exhibitions at Berry-Hill Galleries. He is the organizer of the Sunday Unorganicized reading at ABC NO RIO on the Lower East Side, producer of the Alternative New Year's Day Spoken Word/Performance Extravaganza, and editor of *Stained Sheets*. Since 1996, he has been a member of the spoken word/music performance group Bruce Weber's No Chance Ensemble, which performs regularly in the New York area.

ARTURO RODRÍGUEZ: Born in Las Villas, Cuba in 1956, Rodriguez was exiled to Madrid, Spain with his family in 1971. His work is included in numerous prestigious collections, among them The Metropolitan Museum of Art and The Israel Museum in Jerusalem. Since 1996, the Smithsonian's Archives of American Art has been collecting his drawings, catalogues and correspondence. He has had solo and group exhibitions at museums and galleries in France, Spain, Switzerland, Colombia, Mexico, Panama and the United States.

JOANNE PAGANO WEBER spent her childhood in the Bronx where a matriarchal tradition of storytelling became a lifelong influence, evident still in her paintings, drawings, sets and writing. Presently she is a textile designer in New York City and lives in Queens with her husband Bruce Weber and their two cats Venus and Lea. She is a member of Bruce Weber's No Chance Ensemble which she currently directs.

of course, that abilities do not evolve unless objective conditions are favorable." [6] Sartre cannot accept such a definition.

Sartre's ontological conception of freedom is not a description of those conditions external to man which allow him to choose among alternatives but, rather, freedom is the state of Being of the *pour-soi* to which the *pour-soi* is condemned. "We are a freedom which chooses, but we do not choose to be free: we are condemned to freedom." [7] Since the *pour-soi* is in question in its Being, freedom is its condition: "I am . . . an existant which *learns of* its freedom by its acts . . . My freedom is perpetually in question in my being; it is not a super-added quality or a *property* of my nature; it is the very stuff of my being." [8]

To comprehend freedom is to understand that the human reality is its own Nothingness.[9] The *pour-soi*, in order to be, must choose itself. There is no *a priori* essence or God-given human nature that the *pour-soi* can depend upon or cling to. The *pour-soi* is "entirely abandoned, without aid of any sort, to the unbearable necessity of making itself be down to the slightest detail." [10]

Man's freedom cannot be relative to any particular situation or occurrence; for his freedom is his Nothingness, and his Nothingness is an absolute in the sense that it is the condition of the *pour-soi*. Thus, "man could not be sometimes free and sometimes slave: he is entirely and always free, or he is not." [11]

2. SITUATION

Thus far freedom has been described in terms of the "lack" of the *pour-soi*. However, it is necessary to understand the *pour-soi* not as an

[6] McGill, V. J., "Sartre's Doctrine of Freedom," *Revue Internationale de Philosophie*, (15 Juillet 1949), 341.

[7] EN, 565.

[8] *Ibid.*, 514.

[9] *Ibid.*, 515. "To be, for the *pour-soi*, is to nihilate the *en-soi* which it is. In these conditions, freedom could be nothing other than this nihilation. It is through it that the *pour-soi* escapes its being as its essence; it is through it that the *pour-soi* is always something other than what one can *say* of it, for . . . the *pour-soi* is that which is already beyond the name one gives to it, the property one recognizes in it. To say that the *pour-soi* has to be what it is; to say that it is what it is not in notbeing what it is; to say that in it existence precedes and conditions essence or . . . that for it '*Wesen ist was gewesen ist*,' is to say one sole and selfsame thing, namely, that man is free."

[10] *Ibid.*, 516.

[11] *Ibid.*

abstraction but as *engaged,* as *in situation.* In fact, the *pour-soi is* only in so far as it is engaged and in situation. We must, therefore, turn to the concept of situation in order to describe the more profound implications of Sartre's theory of human freedom.

The situation of man is the totality of the limits with which the *pour-soi* is faced in its relation to the world. This world consists of other *pour-sois* and of things. Although the objective world of "brute things" "may, from the start, limit our freedom of action, it is our freedom itself which must previously constitute the framework, the technique, and the ends in regard to which they will manifest themselves as limits." [12]

The situation, then, is the resultant or synthesis of two aspects of reality: the facticity of things as revealed in their coefficient of adversity, and the meanings which the *pour-soi* legislates for them. The relation of the *pour-soi* to a situation is described through what Sartre terms "being-there." "Being-there for a colonial is to be twenty days from France—better still: if he is a functionary and awaits his paid voyage, it is to be six months and seven days from Bordeaux." [13] It is through being-there that the object of desire or of cognition takes on meaning for the *pour-soi*; and its meaning identifies the situation and defines it. The mountain I now look at has a certain "coefficient of adversity." It *is* difficult to climb, it *is* high, it *is* craggy, etc.; but the meaning of "difficult to climb" and of "high" and of "craggy" is determined by the *pour-soi* who is confronted by that mountain in a particular situation.[14]

The relationship between situation and freedom is one of paradox. Freedom exists only in a situation and a situation exists only if the *pour-soi* is free. "The human reality encounters everywhere resistances and obstacles which it has not created; but these resistances and these

---

[12] EN, 562.

[13] *Ibid.,* 574.

[14] *Ibid.,* 569. "To an equal desire to climb, the rock will be easy to ascend for such an athletic climber, difficult for such another, a novice badly trained and with a puny body. But the body reveals itself in its turn as well or badly trained only in regard to a free choice. It is because I am there and have made of myself what I am that the rock develops in regard to my body a coefficient of adversity. For the lawyer living in town who pleads, for the body hidden under his legal robe, the rock is neither difficult nor easy to ascend: it is melted into the totality 'world' without emerging in any way from it."

obstacles have meaning only in and through the free choice which *is* the human reality." [15]

But situation is itself partially a function of the *pour-soi* which is understood under the dimensions of temporality: past, present, and future. Hence, a situation will be constituted, in part, by what I *was* as well as by what I *am*. If *"Wesen ist was gewesen ist,"* then the past can be understod only in paradox. "I could not conceive of myself without a past; better, I could no longer *think* anything about myself since I think about what I *am*, and I am in the past; but on the other hand, I am the being through which the past comes to itself and to the world." [16]

Sartre's conception of situation and freedom as intimately associated and correlative aspects of the *pour-soi* defines the nature of human reality. "If the *pour-soi* is nothing other than its situation, it follows that the being-in-situation defines the human reality." [17] However, it must be stressed that while the *pour-soi* expresses its existence in situation, the situation is not solely constituted by the *pour-soi*. The *pour-soi* is thrown into a world which consists of other *pour-sois* and their situations. The other *pour-sois* have established meanings in the world which then function as part of the reality which surrounds the individual *pour-soi*.[18]

Thus, to be free is "not to choose the historical world in which one arises—which would have no sense—but to choose oneself in the world, whatever it may be." [19] The realistic element in Sartre is apparent: the *pour-soi* does not create the world in any Fichtean sense. There is, rather, a given which the *pour-soi* grasps and, in grasping, renders uniquely meaningful to itself. "Freedom . . . recognizes and foresees implicitly in its original project the independent existence of the given on which it exercises itself." [20]

---

[15] EN, 569.

[16] *Ibid.*, 577–578. "Let us examine this paradox more closely: freedom being choice is change. It defines itself by the end which it projects, that is, by the future which it has to be. But precisely because the future is *the-state-which-is-not-yet* of that *which is*, it can be conceived only in a direct liaison to that which is. And it could not be that which is what clarifies that which is not yet: for that which is is *lack* and, consequently, cannot be known as such except from that which it lacks."

[17] *Ibid.*, 634.

[18] *Ibid.*, 603.

[19] *Ibid.*, 604.

[20] *Ibid.*, 588.

The complexus of choice-freedom-lack-nothingness-situation, which *is* the *pour-soi* as it "exists" itself, is ultimately reducible to two basic aspects: the given and the ends which the *pour-soi* imposes upon the given. "The arising of freedom is a crystallization of an end *through a given*, and discovery of a given in the light of an end: these two structures are simultaneous and inseparable." [21]

3. DEATH

Sartre asserts that it is not possible for the *pour-soi* to be aware of its own possibility of dying. *My* death must in principle remain outside the orbit of my comprehension. "Death is not *my* possibility of no longer realizing a presence in the world, but *an always possible nihilation of my possibles, which is outside of my possibility.*" [22]

Sartre is quite willing to admit that the *pour-soi* can imagine *a* death, but not *its* death.[23] *My* death is a comprehensible notion only for the Other. "The *fact of death* . . . gives final victory to the point of view of the Other." [24] Sartre maintains that since, in principle, death, in so far as it is *my* death, is comprehended by the Other, my death can never be for me an ontological structure. It is unanalyzable and beyond me.[25]

It is now possible to see that there are two basic existential characteristics which qualify the *pour-soi*: "nothing is in the consciousness which is not consciousness of Being," and, secondly, "my Being is in question in my Being—which means that nothing comes to me which is not chosen." [26] These characteristics determine a *pour-soi* which, through the aspects of "lack," choice, Nothingness, etc., "exists" itself as freedom. This freedom is a strictly ontological concept. It is not to be confused with what is ordinarily meant by freedom. Sartre thus has given us a radically new concept of freedom: the *pour-soi's* situation or status as it "exists" itself ontologically. Freedom is the necessary condition of the *pour-soi*, and is evidenced in the *pour-soi* in so far as the *pour-soi* exists as "lack." Such is the freedom to which the *pour-soi* is condemned.

[21] EN, 590.
[22] *Ibid.*, 621.
[23] *Ibid.*, 624.
[24] *Ibid.*, 628.
[25] *Ibid.*, 630.
[26] *Ibid.*, 578.

Chapter IV

EXISTENTIAL PSYCHOANALYSIS

1. EXISTENTIAL VERSUS FREUDIAN PSYCHOANALYSIS

Sartre defines existential psychoanalysis as a "special phenomenological method,"[1] a "method designed to bring to light, under a rigorously objective form, the subjective choice by which each person makes himself a person, that is, makes himself announce to himself what he is."[2] The existential psychoanalyst rejects the Freudian psychoanalysis in so far as the latter describes certain general 'states' (complexes, attitudes, etc.) rather than individually determined projects and choices. The goal of existential psychoanalysis is to reveal the symbolization and rapports contained in the projects of the *pour-soi* and to find "through these empirical and concrete projects the original manner which each one has of choosing his being."[3]

How does existential psychoanalysis differ from phenomenological ontology? The answer to this question will clarify the differences between orthodox and existential psychoanalyses. For Sartre, ontology has as its aim the analysis of the structure of Being in general. It cannot attempt a study of the detailed history of an individual *pour-soi*; it cannot make predictions concerning the outcome of any specific situation. These particularized questions are the concern of existential psychoanalysis.

The existential psychoanalysis interrogates particular human conducts, tendencies, inclinations, etc., and attempts to "decipher" their existential meaning. The principle of this kind of psychoanalysis is that man is comprehended as a totality, not as a collection of separate facts. Every act of man, however insignificant it may seem, reveals something of his nature. The goal of this psychoanalysis is to "decipher" the empirical behavior of man. It is primarily through a de-

---

[1] EN, 559.
[2] *Ibid.*, 662.
[3] *Ibid.*, 689.

tailed and complete analysis of the acts of choice which a man makes that the existential psychoanalyst may hope to formulate a picture of the relationship between specific choices of an individual and the symbolic meanings which those choices represent.

The essential difference between the existential and the Freudian psychoanalyses is that the latter stresses the general complexes and attitudes determined unconsciously in the individual, while the former holds that all mental conditions are consciously disclosed and are to be comprehended through an analysis of the situation of the person. The two psychoanalyses are in closest agreement in regard to fundamental method and the desirability of reconstructing the total picture of the individual mind through an exhaustive investigation of the individual's personal history and behavior.[4]

2. EXISTENTIAL PSYCHOANALYSIS AND ONTOLOGY

Ontology lays the groundwork for general and abstract significations which analyze the nature of Being. Existential psychoanalysis is a method of applying the basic ontological principles to highly individualized projects, i.e., of analyzing the specific attitudes and actions of the individual in relation to his life-history. In this respect, ontology is basic to existential psychoanalysis: "The information which ontology may acquire about conducts and desire must serve as principles of existential psychoanalysis." [5] Thus, "What ontology may teach psychoanalysis is, in effect, first of all the *true* origin of the significations of things and their *true* relation to the human reality." [6]

3. VISCOSITY

Sartre investigates the structure and basis of the existential psychoanalysis but is interested in describing the method rather than in using it. However, he does give us some illustrative examples of how he intends to apply the method. While Sartre's *Baudelaire* is a full length study in existential psychoanalysis, its consideration would involve us in too great a digression from the issues with which we have been dealing. We will therefore restrict ourselves to the analysis of "viscocity," which is the most extended illustration of existential psychoanalysis in EN.

---

[4] EN, 656–658.
[5] *Ibid.*, 663.
[6] *Ibid.*, 694.

The analysis of viscosity is indebted to Bachelard's attempted psychoanalysis of things.[7] Bachelard holds that one may psychoanalyze things, such as water, stones, fire, etc. Sartre is sympathetic toward this notion but holds that Bachelard's work lacked the method necessary to carry out a successful analysis of things.[8]

Sartre's analysis of viscosity is an application of the principles of existential psychoanalysis to things; but in the case of viscosity the things are of prime importance, since viscosity is symbolic of the *en-soi*, and to penetrate its nature is to know the nature of the *en-soi*.

The "viscous" is the sticky, glue-like, tar-like, soft quicksand-like stuff that was best described earlier in Sartre's novel *Nausea*.[9] But the viscous is not simply matter: "a handshake is viscous, a smile is viscous, a thought, a sentiment is capable of being viscous." [10] We know the nature of the viscous when we consider it in its relation to the *pour-soi*. This relationship is dual: on the one hand, the viscous is molded by us, shaped by us; on the other hand, it "seizes" us and possesses us.[11]

The possibility of losing mastership over the viscous "haunts" the *pour-soi*, for "the viscous is the revenge of the en-soi." [12] The fear of the *pour-soi* that it will be absorbed by the *en-soi* is the essence of the "flight" of the *pour-soi* previously described by Sartre.[13]

---

[7] EN, 694.

[8] *Ibid.*, "We would consider the study of Bachelard on water, which teems with ingenious and profound insights, as an ensemble of suggestions, as a precious collection of materials which would have to be utilized at present by a psycholoanalysis conscious of its principles."

[9] Vide supra 29–30.

[10] EN, 695.

[11] *Ibid.*, 700. "The viscous is *docile*. Only, at the very moment when I believe to possess it, by a curious reversal, it is *it* which possesses me. It is there that appears its essential character: its softness makes a suction. If the object that I hold in my hand is solid, I am able to let it slip when it pleases me; its inertia symbolizes for me my entire power: I found it, but it never founds me . . . here it is that the viscous reverses the terms: the *pour-soi* is suddenly compromised. I remove my hands, I wish to let go of the viscous but it adheres to me, it sucks me, it clings to me; its mode of being is neither the reassuring inertia of a solid, nor a dynamism as that of water which wears itself out sliding away from me: it is a soft activity, frothy and feminine of suction, it lives obscurely under my fingers and I sense it as a dizziness, it attracts me . . . as the bottom of an abyss would be able to attract me. It is like a tactile fascination of the viscous. I am no longer the master of *stopping* the process of appropriation."

[12] *Ibid.*, 701.

[13] *Ibid.*, 702.

The existential psychoanalysis of the viscous, Sartre claims, has revealed a sector of Being. We know *en-soi* through our experience of the viscous in nausea, and this experience suggests "a crowd of obscure significations and of sendings-back which pass beyond it." [14] In its most profound sense, the viscous "is a possible meaning of Being." [15]

[14] EN, 703.
[15] *Ibid.*

Chapter V

GENERAL SUMMARY

"For us, man is defined first of all as a being 'in a situation.'
That means that he forms a synthetic whole with his situation
—biological, economic, political, cultural, etc. He cannot be dis-
tinguished from his situation, for it forms him and decides his
possibilities; but, inversely, it is he who gives it meaning by
making his choices within it and by it. To be in a situation, as
we see it, is to choose oneself in a situation, and men differ from
one another in their situations and also in the choices they them-
selves make of themselves. What men have in common is not a
"nature" but a condition, that is, an ensemble of limits and re-
strictions: The inevitablity of death, the necessity of working for
a living, of living in a world already inhabited by other men.
Fundamentally this condition is nothing more than the basic
human situation, or, if you prefer, the ensemble of abstract char-
acteristics common to all situations."

—Sartre

The topics to be discussed as general conclusions are Sartre's ideas
regarding "situation," his explanation of how the dualism of Being
(*en-soi* and *pour-soi*) is bridged, his statements regarding metaphysical
questions, and, finally, his views on moral matters.

1. APPROPRIATION

Human reality for Sartre is understood only through *situation*.
The *pour-soi* is not isolated in its existence; rather, it is engaged with
the totality of things, Others, etc., which establishes the *pour-soi* as a
being-in-the-midst-of-things. While I am "absolutely free and responsi-
ble for my situation . . . I am never free *except in a situation*." [1]

---

[1] EN, 590.

Since without the *pour-soi* there cannot be a situation, it is the *pour-soi* which constitutes its reality. By being-in-the-world the *pour-soi* is responsible for legislating significance to the world in which it is. It is here, then, that the relationship between the situation and man's freedom is made clear:

> "Man, being condemned to be free, carries the weight of the world on his shoulders: he is responsibile for the world and for himself considered as manner of being. . . . The responsibility of the *pour-soi* is overwhelming, since it is that through which *there is* a world; and, since it is also that which *makes itself be,* whatever may be the situation in which it finds itself, the *pour-soi* must assume this situation entirely . . . with the proud consciousness of being the author of it. . . . The situation is *mine* . . . because it is the image of my free choice of myself and all that it presents to me is *mine* in that it represents me and symbolizes me." [2]

However, the realistic element in Sartre's conception of situation must be stressed. The *pour-soi* does not of itself create its world; rather, in reacting to objective givens (objects, Others, significations created by Others, etc.), it makes of these givens the world of meanings it both "exists" and exists in. The brute given is nothing without the testimonies of Others and their significations.[3]

In the same manner, my past actions are never wholly completed and accomplished facts alone. In addition to the brute fact of their pastness, the meaning which they have is continually dependent on the significance which I continue to give them.[4]

---

[2] EN, 639.

[3] *Ibid.,* 579.

[4] *Ibid.,* 579. "The signification of the past is narrowly dependent on my present project. That signifies by no means that I am able to vary at the mercy of my caprices the meaning of my anterior acts; but, much to the contrary, that the fundamental project that I am decides absolutely the signification which the past that *I* have to be can have for me and for others. I alone in fact am able to decide at each moment the burden of the past: not in discussing, in deliberating, and in appreciating in each case the importance of such and such an anterior event, but in projecting myself toward my goals, I save the past with me and I *decide* by action its signification. Who shall decide if that mystic crisis of my fifteenth year 'was' pure accident of puberty or, on the contrary, first sign of a future conversion. I, according as I shall decide— at twenty, at thirty—to convert myself. The project of conversion confers at one sole stroke upon a crisis of adolescence the value of a premonition that I had not taken seriously."

In regard to the facticity of pastness, the conclusion is that although "all my past is there, pressing, urgent, imperious," still "I choose its meaning." [5] The past is never 'settled' once and for all, but the meaning of the past is perpetually in "suspension." [6] The meaning of the past is clarified only in the context of my present situation, and so Sartre terms this active, unstable past the "is-was" (*est été*).[7]

Despite the realistic element of the world (as expressed in the coefficient of adversity of things, the significations due to Others, the historical past, etc.), situation is primarily an expression of the active role of the *pour-soi* in fashioning the world which it "exists." The world is revealed to me, and, in this sense, I am its creator and possessor.[8]

The key concept which explains how situation is an expression of the *pour-soi* is what Sartre terms "appropriation." In appropriation the *pour-soi* gives meaning to its reality; it molds the significations for which it is responsible; the *pour-soi* "exists" its significations.

The concept of appropriation leads beyond constitution of meanings to an understanding of the special status of the *pour-soi*, for the *pour-soi is* the human reality. Its priority over facticity engenders the necessary interpretation that the existence of reality is a function of the *pour-soi*, and that it can be grasped only in the situation which the *pour-soi* "exists":

> "To the degree to which I appear to myself as *creating* the objects through the sole rapport of appropriation, these objects are *I*. The pen and the pipe, the article of clothing, the desk, the house, *it is I*. The totality of my possessions reflects the totality of my being. I *am* what I *have. It is I* that I touch on this cup, on this trinket. This mountain which I climb, *it is I* to the degree to which I conquer it; and when I am at its summit, which I have 'acquired' at the price of some efforts, this large view over the valley and the surrounding mountains, *it is I*; the panorama, it is I expanded to the horizon, for it exists only through me, only for me." [9]

[5] EN, 580.
[6] *Ibid.*, 582.
[7] "is-was" is another of Sartre's ungrammatical constructions. There seems to be no other way of successfully rendering the meaning of this term in English.
[8] *Ibid*, 666.
[9] *Ibid.*, 680–681.

Through the appropriation I "egotize" my reality. The mountain which is I is not "within" me in any sense; rather, it is I externalized. "Possession is a magic rapport; I *am* these objects which I possess, but outside of all subjectivity as an *en-soi* which escapes me at each instant and whose creation I perpetuate at each instant." [10]

Appropriation is thus a paradoxical concept, for it seeks to explain both the realistic (objective) factor in experience and the idealistic (subjective) aspect which is the *pour-soi*. It amounts, in analytic reduction, to the problem of the *en-soi–pour-soi*—an ideal and un-realizable concept.[11]

In so far as appropriation leads ultimately to the problem of the *en-soi–pour-soi,* we are returned to the very question of EN: the problem of the nature of Being; for the *en-soi–pour-soi* is absolute Being. However, since the *en-soi–pour-soi* is an ideal and unrealizable structure, the question arises, How can appropriation be the project of the *en-soi–pour-soi*? The answer is that appropriation symbolizes the essential nature of the existant who, as *pour-soi,* can never be his own proper foundation, who, as Nothingness, is in flight toward an *en-soi* which he can never attain.[12]

2. THE DUALISM OF EN-SOI AND POUR-SOI

Since appropriation is symbolic of the ideal but impossible *en-soi-pour-soi,* the basic dualism of *en-soi* and *pour-soi* is still unresolved. In yearning to be its own foundation, the *pour-soi* seeks the status of *en-soi–pour-soi*: the Absolute. Another name for this Absolute is God. The ideal of *en-soi–pour-soi* is the ideal of "a consciousness which would be foundation of its own being-*en-soi* by the pure consciousness that it would take of itself.[13] The *pour-soi,* if it could achieve this ideal status, would be God. "Thus," Sartre writes, "one can say that what renders the fundamental project of the human reality most con-ceivable is the fact that man is that being who projects himself to be God." [14]

---

[10] EN, 681.
[11] *Ibid.,* 682.
[12] *Ibid.,* 682.
[13] *Ibid.,* 653.
[14] *Ibid.*

Sartre concludes that "to be man is to stretch toward being God; or, if one prefers, man is fundamentally desire to be God." [15] That man is condemned to the desire to be God is his tragic condition. The dialectic of relationships between *pour-soi* and *en-soi* is the profound description of this failure to achieve the Absolute. Sartre states the conclusion of the *en-soi–pour-soi* dialectic: each human reality seeks to metamorphose its own *pour-soi* into *en-soi–pour-soi*, but in striving for this status, the *pour-soi* must lose itself if it makes itself *en-soi*. The projection of the *pour-soi* to lose itself in order to found its own Being Sartre terms a "passion." But since the status of *en-soi–pour-soi* is impossible for the *pour-soi* to attain—since man cannot be God—the *pour-soi* loses itself in vain: "man is a useless passion." [16]

Having spent the main part of EN in describing the nature of the two polarities of Being and in analyzing the flight of the *pour-soi* as well as the ideal but unrealizable *en-soi–pour-soi,* Sartre concludes his work by returning to the original question of whether the polarities of Being constitute an irrevocably separate and distinct dualism whose members can never be unified. He seeks to establish an ultimate resolution of the dualism: "the *pour-soi* and the *en-soi* are reunited by a synthetic liaison which is not other than the *pour-soi* itself." [17]

The *pour-soi,* then, is considered as "synthetic liaison" which unites the *en-soi* and the *pour-soi*. This union, however, is to be understood in regard to the genesis of the dualism. We mean simply that Sartre's answer to the dualism is really an answer to the question: How did the dualities arise? It is not an answer to the question: In what manner may the *pour-soi* unite itself with the *en-soi*? Sartre says that ontology cannot answer this latter question, for "we do not have grounds to interrogate ourselves about the manner in which the *pour-soi* may unite itself to the *en-soi* since the *pour-soi* is in no way an autonomous substance." [18] The only substance which the *pour-soi* has is its Nothingness.

3. METAPHYSICAL QUESTIONS

Further investigation of the problem of the dualism of Being leads to metaphysical considerations. Sartre says that the metaphysical

---

[15] EN, 653–654.
[16] *Ibid.,* 708.
[17] *Ibid.,* 711.
[18] *Ibid.,* 712.

problem might be formulated in this way: Why does the *pour-soi* arise from Being? [19] Since, for Sartre, the ontological investigation is by definition a phenomenological study, we can analyze only givens; we cannot turn to questions of the ultimate origin of givens. It is the task of metaphysics to take up where, because of its method, ontology must leave off.

4. ETHICAL QUESTIONS

A final area of philosophic inquiry is taken up in the conclusion of EN: the question of ethical values. Sartre asserts that ontology is not concerned directly with formulating moral prescriptions. Ontology "concerns itself uniquely with that which is, and it is not possible to derive imperatives from indicatives." [20] It is possible to indicate, however, the general lines along which an existential ethic might be formulated. The existential ethic will begin its analysis by studying the human being as a *pour-soi* in a situation. Since, for Sartre, all values are determined through the choices that the *pour-soi* makes, it follows that the *pour-soi* will be understood as creating its moral values through its acts. The moral agent is "the being through whom values exist." [21] The existential analysis of values will be based upon the categories of Being, Nothingness, freedom, anguish, and so on, as these categories have been clarified through phenomenological ontology. The existential ethic will be founded upon a freedom which will "take consciousness of itself and will discover itself in anguish as the unique source of value." [22]

The multiple questions and difficulties which face such an ethic are problems to be met in a special and separate work which Sartre promises in the closing line of EN. This work on existential ethics has not yet appeared.

[19] EN, 713.
[20] *Ibid.*, 720.
[21] *Ibid.*, 722.
[22] *Ibid.*

PART II
Evaluation

Chapter VI

SARTRE'S PHENOMENOLOGICAL METHOD

In any analysis of *L'Être et le Néant,* it is imperative that Sartre's use of phenomenological method be considered and evaluated. It is not a coincidence that phenomenology appears in Sartre's ontology, for we have been advised in the subtitle of EN, "Essay in Phenomenological Ontology," of his intention to make use of the phenomenological method. Since Sartre appears to mean by phenomenology the special discipline formulated by Husserl, it will be well to begin our discussion with a brief resumé of Husserl's position.

Husserl's early interests were in mathematics—more specifically, in so-called "foundations of mathematics." His first basic problem was one of "reconciling the objective validity of logic and mathematics with the subjective processes of experiencing."[1] Prior to Husserl's work on this problem there was a strong tradition which held that logic is intimately related to psychology, that logic is really a sub-branch of psychology. Various writers argued that meaning and truth are dependent upon psychological processes, and that logical validity is possible only in so far as it is grounded in the thought-processes of individuals. According to Lipps, for example, "the rules of correct thought are identical with the natural laws of thought itself; and logic is either the physics of thought or nothing at all." [2] This "psychologism" Husserl examined; and to its refutation he devoted his first philosophical efforts.

The essence of Husserl's refutation of psychologism consists in his demonstration of the *a priori* validity of logical laws; i.e., it consists in demonstrating that the laws of logic are "established through apodictic evidence and not inductively." [3] As Husserl sees it, psychology, "because of its inability to yield more than empirical generalities, . . .

[1] Farber, M., *The Foundation of Phenomenology,* 561.
[2] *Ibid.,* 110.
[3] *Ibid.,* 112.

cannot account for the apodictically evident, 'superempirical,' ab-solutely exact laws which make up the core of logic." [4] By pointing out the "ideal" nature of logical necessity, Husserl undermined the foundation of that psychologism according to which logical necessity is derived from "matters of fact." [5]

The refutation of psychologism leads Husserl later in his career to the formulation of the distinctive philosophic method which is known as phenomenology. Husserl was able to "break through" to pheno-menology largely because in his work on psychologism he had raised certain key questions for which, at that time, no method of philoso-phizing could provide an answer. These key questions were con-cerned with the attempt to relate subjectivity (not psychologistically understood) to those meanings, logical unities, and "ideal" elements in experience which Husserl had described in his attempt to rescue logic from psychology; they were questions concerning the possibility of exploring subjectivity in a non-psychologistic manner. In his pre-phenomenlogical period Husserl faced the problem of the " 'clarifica-tion' of the fundamental concepts of logic and mathematics, and of their relationship to thought processes." [6] In his phenomenological period, Husserl expanded this problem into a larger one: the search for a transcendental phenomenology which would provide a "uni-versal . . . method for philosophy and a final foundation for science." [7]

> "The aim of phenomenological analysis," Farber writes, "is to bring the logical concepts and laws to epistemological clarity and distinctness. The logical concepts as valid thought-unities must originate in intuition, and must arise through 'ideating abstraction' on the basis of certain experiences. In repeated performances of this abstraction the logical concepts must be always confirmed anew, and must be grasped in their self-

[4] Farber, M., *op. cit.*, 112.

[5] *Ibid.*, 114: "An analysis of the real meaning of logical laws shows that they are not laws of actual mental life. The psychologistic interpretation therefore does violence to the meaning of logical laws, which do not presuppose the facts of mental life, either in their content or in their establishment, any more than is the case in pure mathematics. The valid forms of inference refer generally to any terms or propositions, and do not involve the existence of any actual judgments or psychical phenomena."

[6] Farber, M., "Phenomenology," *Twentieth Century Philosophy*, 350.

[7] *Ibid.*

identity. Expressed otherwise: Husserl is not content with 'mere words,' or with a merely symbolic understanding of words, such as we have to begin with in our reflections about the meaning of the laws set up in pure logic regarding 'concepts,' 'judgments,' 'truths,' etc. Meanings which are only animated by remote, confused, figurative intuitions—if by any at all—cannot satisfy him. He proposes to return to the 'things themselves.' By means of fully developed intuitions we are to see with evidence that what is given here in actually performed abstraction is really and truly that which word-meanings of the law mean." [8]

The cry of "back to the things themselves" is the attempt to devise a philosophy which will take a new attitude toward the examination of the content of experience. This new attitude is at once the attempt to construct a "presuppositionless" method and a philosophy which will begin with that "root" experience or givenness which neither reflection nor dialectic nor scientific disciplines of any order can meaningfully deny.

> "The 'phenomenology' represented by the *Logical Investigations* makes use of immanent intuition alone, and does not pass beyond the sphere of the intuitively given. That is the meaning of the precept 'Back to the things themselves'; it meant the appeal to intuitive givenness." [9]

The question now is: What sort of attitude are we leaving when we turn to phenomenology, and what sort of attitude may we expect from phenomenology? The answers Husserl gives to these questions are clear. The phenomenological attitude is a radical departure from what Husserl termed the "natural" attitude—a term denoting the common-sense, uncritical view of the world which accepts as "obvious" the existence of things, of other persons, and of a structure of meanings which relate ourselves to the world we live in: In the phenomenological attitude nothing can be taken for granted. The presuppositions of the natural attitude are among the very elements to be explained by phenomenological philosophy.

Husserl's method is essentially a return in principle to the Cartesian point of view. Phenomenological knowledge must begin in subjectivity via the reflections of the meditating ego. Thus:

---

[8] Farber, M., *The Foundation of Phenomenology*, 213.
[9] *Ibid.*, 218.

"The choice of a subjective method is due to the aim for complete and *radical* understanding, which is of deciding importance for philosophy. Nothing may be naively assumed; there must be no pre-judgments. In the natural view of the world, the common-sense view, and in all the special sciences, a general thesis of existence is taken to be obvious. Its unconscious acceptance is well justified for purposes of natural existence, but not for theoretical understanding. A world existing continuously and independently of our experiencing is the natural basis for non-philosophic thinking. But because philosophy is guided by the ideal of completeness of understanding, it cannot allow even so obvious a belief to remain unquestioned. The 'natural' view of the world after all contains elements of theoretical interpretation to which we have become accustomed. In short, everything must be questioned, including the phenomenological procedure itself. Hence only a subjectivistic method which begins with the experiencing knower and his evidence will answer." [10]

The first step in phenomenological investigation is a "reduction" of our common or "natural" experience into those special aspects of experience which are the objects of phenomenological investigation. As Farber points out, this "reduction"

"is really twofold, and consists of (1) eidetic reduction, which means that only essences, or essential structures, are of interest, and not particular facts; and (2) transcendental reduction, with its technique of 'elimination' and 'bracketing,' which leads one back to the 'pure' consciousness of an individual knower as the starting-point for philosophy." [11]

In the transcendental reduction (termed "epoché") all judgments about existence, including material things, are suspended, placed in abeyance. The objects to which these judgments refer are bracketed, or put in quotation marks. What is left after this reduction are the perceiving, remembrances, and imaginings of the experiencing being. The bracketed world becomes a phenomenon for a transcendentally reduced consciousness.[12] The reduction, which is the essence of the phenomenological attitude, thus enables the phenomenologist to go back to the "originary given."

---

[10] Farber, M., "Phenomenology," *op. cit.*, 350–351.

[11] *Ibid.*, 353.

[12] *Ibid.*, 353.

The nature of the starting point of phenomenology, the nature of the objects with which phenomenology is concerned—these indicate that Husserl's transcendental procedure is an attempt to examine the lowest categorial level of experience; and at this level the primary structure of subjectivity is, in Husserl's terminology, "intentionality." Consciousness, for Husserl, would not be consciousness were it not consciousness *of something*. Consciousness *intends*. Via its acts of intention it "endows" objects with meaning. Husserl's investigations of intentionality aim at a clarification of the complex relationships which prevail between the *cogito* and the meaning-intentions of the *cogito,* and open up a vast nexus of problems which, since they are basic to subjectivity, are basic to practically every area of human experience—basic to every discipline and to the structure of science. Phenomenology, therefore, as practiced by Husserl is but a prolegomenon to all branches of science and philosophy.

"The aim of phenomenology is said to be the achievement of an 'absolute knowledge of the world,' which it attempts to accomplish by going beyond all 'worldly' forms of explanation."[13] Phenomenology "seeks to point out all presuppositions" and views everything factual as an exemplification of essential structures." It "is not concerned with matters of fact as such,"[14] but with the "originarily given" in the "stream of pure experience." [15]

Now Sartre, despite the fact that he speaks of his inquiry as "phenomenological," nowhere asserts that he is a "phenomenologist" following Husserl's method in detail. On the contrary, we shall show that Sartre departs radically from Husserl's method and that the term "phenomenological," when applied to Sartre's method, is ambiguous and, in certain respects, a misnomer.

The "phenomenological" basis of EN is contained in the first 37 pages of the book. It is in these pages that Sartre discusses the idea of phenomena, the phenomena of Being and the Being of phenomena, the pre-reflective *cogito,* and other relevant matters. He is attempting to do two things: (1) to concretize, locate, and, in general, indicate the problem of Being; (2) to show the initial differentiation of Being into two regions which are ultimately defined as the *en-soi* and the *pour-soi.*

---

[13] Farber, M., *The Foundation of Phenomenology,* 547.
[14] *Ibid.,* 568.
[15] *Ibid.,* 353.

In attempting to develop the fundamental dualism which permeates the whole of his ontology, Sartre, early in EN, discusses the seemingly dualistic terms of the phenomena of Being and the Being of phenomena.[16] Again, the primary consideration of the *cogito* and of consciousness as later contrasted with the treatment of being *en-soi* is another aspect of Sartre's technique of setting up the dualism of his ontology, since consciousness resides in the *pour-soi*. What is the phenomenological basis for the derivation and analysis of these structures?

Sartre tells us that "being is neither a quality of the object seizable among others, nor a sense of the object. The object does not reflect back to being as to a signification." [17] We learn, further, that "the object does not *possess* being, and its existence is not a participation in being, nor any other kind of relation. It *is*, that is the sole manner of defining its way of being." [18] The object can neither conceal nor reveal Being, since there is no hidden Being behind the appearance of the object. The object, rather than revealing itself to us, is there to-be-revealed. Sartre says: "Being is simply the condition of all revealing; it is being-in-order-to-reveal and not being revealed." [19] The Being of the phenomenon constitutes the transphenomenality of Being. We are able to have knowledge of this transphenomenality of Being since it is coextensive with the phenomenon of Being and makes itself known to us by an "overflowing." [20]

Our basic criticism of this analysis of Being is that, whatever its merits or insights, it is not a phenomenological analysis. Quite to the contrary, the Husserlian method is put aside as inadequate. To begin with, no *epoché* or reduction has been performed. Sartre holds that the Husserlian reduction is *not* the proper method to begin the analysis of Being, since it is based on the concept of passing beyond particularity to the essence of that particularity. This, according to Sartre,[21] is not a possible method for the analysis of Being, since Being has no meaning or essence 'beyond' its own particularity. Being is to-be-re-

---

[16] Later he will show that the former leads to the region of the *pour-soi* and the latter to the region of the *en-soi*.
[17] EN 15.
[18] *Ibid.*
[19] *Ibid.*
[20] *Ibid.*, 16.
[21] *Ibid.*, 15–16.

vealed, but this revelation is not via any Husserlian phenomenological discipline. Instead, we have what might be termed a quasi-phenomenological sort of method, which may be further described through Sartre's analysis of the *cogito*.

Sartre commences his analysis of consciousness by asserting with Husserl that "all consciousness . . . is consciousness *of* something." [22] In being conscious *of* something, consciousness directs itself outward toward the object of which it is conscious. Thus, the intentional quality is the basic characteristic of the *cogito*. In order for there to be true intention, however, the *cogito* must be self-conscious: "the necessary and sufficient condition for a knowing consciousness to be knowledge of its object is that it be consciousness of itself as being this knowledge." [23] Reflective consciousness in the *cogito* necessitates the precondition of a non-reflective consciousness; this is termed the pre-reflective *cogito*. "It is the non-reflective consciousness which renders the reflections possible: there is a pre-reflective *cogito* which is the condition of the Cartesian *cogito*." [24]

There is no essence of consciousness prior to the intentions of consciousness: "Consciousness is not produced as singular exemplar of an abstract possibility, but . . . in rising from the heart of being it creates and sustains its essence, that is, the synthetic arrangement of its possibilities." [25]

Sartre has argued[26] that Husserl's theory, according to which consciousness is consciousness *of* something, allows of two interpretations: "Either we understand by this that consciousness is constitutive of the being of its object, or else it signifies that consciousness in its most profound nature is in rapport with a transcendent being." [27] Sartre rejects the first interpretation and accepts the second. This is a key point of disagreement with Husserl, since Sartre holds that Husserl's theory of intentionality leads ultimately to a transcendental idealism which makes reality subjectively created and unreal.

[22] EN, 17.
[23] *Ibid.*, 18.
[24] *Ibid.*, 20.
[25] *Ibid.*, 21.
[26] *Ibid.*, 27–29.
[27] *Ibid.*, 27.

"It is in vain that one will attempt a hocus pocus, in basing the *reality* of the object on the subjective impressional plenitude and its objectivity on non-being: never will the objective come out of the subjective, nor the transcendent from the immanent, or being from non-being. But, one will say, Husserl precisely defines consciousness as a transcendence. In fact, it is this which he posits, and it is his essential discovery. But . . . he is totally unfaithful to his principle" [28]

In place of Husserlian phenomenology, Sartre uses a kind of ontological argument. Taking as his point of orientation Husserl's statement that consciousness implies consciousness *of* something, Sartre writes:

"Consciousness is consciousness *of* something: This signifies that transcendence is the constitutive structure of consciousness; i.e., consciousness originates *carried in* a being which is not it. It is this which we call the ontological proof." [29]

Sartre's ontological argument is based on Husserl's theory of intentionality and constitutes an expansion of it:

"To say that consciousness is consciousness of something signifies that for consciousness there is no being outside of this precise obligation to be a revealing intuition of something, i.e., of a transcendent being; . . . for a revealing intuition implies a revealed. Absolute subjectivity can only be constituted in the face of a revealed; immanence can be defined only in the seizure of a transcendent." [30]

Whatever the validity of such ontological arguments, it is necessary to point out that such a form of argumentation is not phenomenological in Husserl's sense of the term. No reduction has been performed; the examined content of subjectivity is thus an unpurified content which bears the marks of the natural attitude. Sartre begins with Husserl's concept of intentionality and divorces it from Husserl's method, losing its methodological precision.

The discussion in the introduction of EN reviewed in the last pages forms Sartre's phenomenological framework for his ontological inquiry.

---

[28] EN, 28.
[29] *Ibid.*
[30] *Ibid.*, 28–29.

With minor exceptions, it is only in the first 37 pages of his 720 page work that he specifically considers any aspects of phenomenology as *method* for philosophizing, and, more specifically, as method for ontological philosophizing; and it is only in these first 37 pages that Sartre makes use of anything resembling Husserlian phenomenology.

We are advised of Sartre's departure from phenomenological techniques in his description of the Other. Since the existence of the Other cannot be determined ontologically, "Sartre . . . renounces all efforts to derive ontologically the existence of the Other."[31] The Other is encountered but not constituted by the ego. We know that the Other exists because he *looks* at us. The importance of noting this inability to give an ontological proof for the existence of the Other is that non-ontological and, in Husserl's sense, non-phenomenological methods of analysis must be used. Thus, those extensive sections in EN dealing with the Other and with the relations to the Other all rest on non-ontological grounds. "Ever since his Ego, in the Third Part of his book, had to acknowledge the existence of the Other as a plain *nécessité de fait,*' his philosophy had left the realm of pure ontology and moved within the onticempirical world." [32]

The nature of Sartre's method may be characterized as quasi-phenomenological and intuitive. The last term needs clarification. Sartre does not use the term "intuition" in the Kantian sense of *Anschauung* but rather in the sense of a *felt* necessity which accompanies an inspection of such experiences as "reveal" themselves as true ontological structures. It is this concept of "revealed" ontological truth which is the heart of Sartre's method. In contrast to hypothetico-deductive types of philosophies, revealed ontology is an exploration of the subject-pole of experience; in contrast to Husserlian phenomenology, ontological revelation does not begin with a formal *epoché* and does not have a precise methodology. If Sartre's ontology is to be characterized as phenomenological, this cannot be done in the sense of Husserl's usage of the term. However, another alternative is open to Sartre to justify his use of the term.

Sartre's only possible justification for describing his procedures as phenomenological is that his is that variety of phenomenology found in Hegel's *Phenomenology of Mind*. In this sense, we ally Sartre's onto-

---

[31] Marcuse, *op. cit.,* 316; also Cf. EN, 307.
[32] *Ibid.,* 319.

logical investigation to the historical genesis of the field of ontology it-self and are enabled to refer the problem of Being back to Hegel and to Aristotle before him. Another alliance which has been quite obvious to students of Sartre is his indebtedness to Heidegger, in whose philosophy the concept of "revelation" is used as the guide to phenomenological method.[33] According to Heidegger, revelation will come through certain modes of experiencing—through certain *moods*; and Sartre takes over much of this concept of "revealing." We can now understand the statement that EN "is in large parts a restatement of Hegel's *Phenomenology of Mind* and Heidegger's *Sein und Zeit*."[34]

Our basic criticism of Sartre's method, then, is that it deserves the name "phenomenological" only in so far as Hegel's phenomenology is intended, and that it is quasi-phenomenological if we are referring to Husserl's variety of phenomenology. Thus, the greatest part of EN is non-phenomenological (in Husserl's sense) and makes use of the intuitive method of "revelation." The specific forms of investigation which characterize the non-phenomenological parts of EN are closest to products of existential psychoanalysis which are on ontic-empirical rather than pure ontological grounds, and are marked by intuitions, projective guesses, literary insights, and psychological analyses. But such existential psychoanalysis is not an inquiry into Being and Nothingness via a phenomenological ontology.

What effect does departure from Husserlian method have on the validity of Sartre's ontology? The answer to this crucial question is reserved for a later time. Meanwhile, it is important to note that Sartre's failure to state clearly his methodological principles and to use Husserlian method, in addition to his failure to give an ontological proof for the existence of the Other and to remain on the grounds of pure ontology for the greater part of EN, results in internal confusions, basic ambiguities, and ultimate contradictions, and, as we hope to show, philosophic failure to resolve his initial problem. The following pages will have as their purpose the criticism of fundamental aspects of Sartre's ontology. We shall attempt to show in detail how the original failure to clarify phenomenological method and to remain within the scope of pure ontology invalidates Sartre's work.

[33] It may be well to remember that Husserl condemned Heidegger's use of phenomenology as a distortion of Husserlian method.

[34] Marcuse, *op. cit.*, 311.

Chapter VII

THREE THESES OF *L'ETRE ET LE NEANT* CRITICIZED

1. FREEDOM

Sartre's concept of freedom is unique: freedom is the condition of the *pour-soi*; and since the *pour-soi* exists as "lack," its freedom is the expression of its Nothingness. The *pour-soi* is what it is not, and is not what it is. This instability defines its freedom. Again, since this *is* the condition of the *pour-soi*, man is condemned to his freedom. Man is condemned to be free because man *is* freedom.

We consider first certain criticisms of Sartre's position.

Emmanuel Mounier argues that since freedom is confined to the circle of subjectivity—to the condition of the *pour-soi*—it never goes beyond its own subjectivity to meet any real objective obstacles, and that it is objectivity which truly defines freedom.

> "Sartre's type of freedom ultimately eschews dramatic appeal, since, in the end, it never actually comes up against any restrictions. Actually, as far as outward observation which objectivates the path taken by freedom is concerned, there is restriction only to the extent to which it is observed. But freedom which is given expression never really comes up against the obstacle, because it creates the obstacle itself, and it never comes up against ultimate limits, not even death, because it has within itself no means of overstepping them. Its limitations are not placed upon it from outside, but by a sort of inherent flabbiness." [1]

Mounier's second point is that Sartre's concept of freedom leads to a form of idealism which excludes any *meaning* from the *pour-soi*:

> "It is impossible to avoid drawing attention to a subtle movement from Realism to ultimate Idealism. Such a drift seems to

---

[1] Mounier, E., *Existentialist Philosophies*, 103.

75

be the result of a form of freedom which, like the whole of human being, does not ultimately represent superabundance of being but poverty of being. It is, in fact, not even being; like the 'for-oneself' with which it is identified, it represents lack of being; it is nothingness. 'It is because human reality is insufficient that it is free.' It is my constant overflow into the nothingness that I am which gives me this nimbleness amongst things; it is my ontological scantiness which makes me so active; it is my aspiration to this gulf of being in me which puts the opportunity and the achievement before me. Freedom does not bring a state of perfection or any meaning into the world; it is nothing but a perpetual inwardization of contingency, nothing but a return to the primitive outburst of absurdity." [2]

His final criticism is that Sartre's concept of freedom leads to a paradoxical theory of responsibility:

"There is . . . a fatal temptation to reduce subjectivity to a form of non-being which is isolated and which gushes forth into the world, which is paradoxically situated in the world and given shape by this fact, but which never actually comes up against the world; it is, in fact, the supreme paradox of a theory of absolute responsibility, a theory by which I am not responsible *in the sight of* anything." [3]

The essence of Mounier's three criticisms is that Sartre is espousing a form of idealism which, in isolating the *pour-soi* from the world and making of it a Nothingness, results in the failure of the *pour-soi* to attain those meanings which come only from real contact with the world. Freedom, meaning, and responsibility are categories applicable to the *pour-soi* only to the degree to which they face objective existence.

These criticisms fail because they rest upon a partial and inadequate interpretation of Sartre's concept of situation. The *pour-soi* is an empty and abstract term without ontological significance unless it is understood, as Sartre intends it to be, in *situation*. Situation is the reality of the *pour-soi*; it is the intense and profound complex of the objective significations, meanings, coefficients of adversity, facticities, etc., determined strictly by Others or by history or by the socio-economic structure of society, and also the activity of the *pour-soi* which legislates *its* unique meaning and interpretation to these objective

[2] Mounier, E., *op. cit.*, 103–104.
[3] *Ibid.*, 104.

structures and relations. Thus, human reality is a combination of objectively existent givens which the *pour-soi* "exists" in the light of the ends and goals by which it defines itself.

In defining itself through choice, the *pour-soi* has a dual role: It meets certain coefficients of adversity (the chains of the slave, for example, and the prison bars which hold him) which it must recognize and admit, but it legislates the meaning of those coefficients of adversity by considering them under certain goals or ideals which it freely chooses (the slave may interpret his chains as elements which limit his liberty or as things to be accepted as his 'just due'; he may interpret his chains as symbols to be revolted against or as symbols to be submitted to, etc.). In choosing the meaning of its coefficient of adversity, the *pour-soi* incorporates the meaning of the obstacle into its situation. In this sense, therefore, the *pour-soi* does meet the obstacles of reality.

The mistake Mounier makes is in asserting that the *pour-soi* does not face reality because it is bound in its subjectivity. But one cannot speak of 'reality' apart from the *pour-soi*, since reality *is* the *pour-soi* in the sense of being the situation of the *pour-soi*. To go beyond the *pour-soi* would be to do one of two things: either to penetrate to some noumenal realm of 'objectivity' or else to realize the status of *en-soi-pour-soi*. Both are impossible for Sartre; the first, because he has shown that there is no *ding-an-sich* 'behind' the phenomenon of Being (appearance *is* Being), and the second, because the whole meaning of the *pour-soi* is that it is what it is not, and is not what it is. Were the *pour-soi* to achieve the status of *en-soi-pour-soi*, the *pour-soi* would be what it is—would become substantialized—and the human reality, as Sartre has described it, would be shattered, for men would not be men but Gods.

The criticism developed by V. J. McGill is colored by the author's naturalist position and presents in clear language those understandable misinterpretations which result from a failure to comprehend the specifically ontological nature of Sartre's inquiry.

We can outline McGill's charges against Sartre's doctrine of freedom as follows:

1. Sartre's assertion that existence precedes essence results in his ignoring the psycho-biological essence of man.[4]

---

[4] McGill, V. J., *op. cit.*, 329–330.

2. The concept of the *pour-soi* as Nothingness is false, since it ignores the basic elements of continuity and stability in man's nature.[5]

3. McGill denies that "for the human-reality, to be is to choose" on the grounds that choice is not the only determinant in being human.[6]

4. In Sartre's assertion "to choose is to be free," choice is a necessary condition of freedom but not a sufficient condition.[7]

5. McGill denies that one becomes intuitively certain of his freedom in his experience of anguish. He analyzes two of Sartre's illustrations: the fear one has in high places that one might hurl himself down, and the anguish the soldier experiences in relation to his future behavior in an attack. Both instances, McGill says, offer feelings of anguish which are not reliable indicators of freedom. He explains the feelings held in such instances as varieties of psychological reactions (panic, auto-suggestibility, etc.) rather than true indicators of freedom.[8]

6. While Sartre's contention is that the "conscious project" rather than past or present events determines our actions, McGill favors the psycho-biological approach to human action and thinks that the work of such behaviorists as Clark Hull will lead to a surer, experimentally-grounded explanation of the problem.[9]

7. Arguing that objective obstacles truly limit man's freedom, McGill opposes what he takes to be Sartre's position on the question, namely, that "obstacles to freedom are only apparent." [10]

8. The conclusion is that Sartre's doctrine of freedom is "too abstract and empty to ever win (*sic.*) general assent," [11] that it does not permit the setting up of criteria of freedom, and, finally, that since it "stipulates that freedom is already universal and inescapable," [12] it cannot give men directives for the extension of their freedom.

McGill's fundamental misinterpretation of Sartre is his failure to realize that Sartre means by the term "freedom" a radically new and

---

[5] McGill, V. J., *op. cit.*, 330–331.
[6] *Ibid.*, 331.
[7] *Ibid.*, 332.
[8] *Ibid.*, 333.
[9] *Ibid.*, 335.
[10] *Ibid.*
[11] *Ibid.*, 341.
[12] *Ibid.*

different doctrine which philosophic analysis has not hitherto revealed. Since Sartre is concerned purely with the ontological nature of freedom, all criticism of his doctrine, if it is to be meaningful, must be oriented with respect to this point of view. McGill, however, starts out with a naturalistic conception of Being and presupposes what Sartre endeavors to analyze.

There are two levels of human freedom: the first is the freedom of human Being which Sartre analyzes. This Being is prior to all psychological pronouncements. The second level of freedom is what naturalists such as McGill have in mind when they use the term. Here freedom refers to the existence of alternatives in human situations: the common sense understanding of freedom. By definition, the slave is the man who does not have freedom; otherwise, he would not be a slave. But the inescapable point is that this definition presupposes the nature of human reality and human consciousness by accepting psychological descriptions which are ontologically unexamined.

Sartre's task is ontological; and with this fact in mind we shall examine the specific charges made by McGill.

1. Sartre does not ignore the psycho-biological basis of man. He describes this basis under the category of "facticity." However, this facticity is not an "essence" of man, since its meaning is dependent upon the *pour-soi* for its interpretation. The *pour-soi* "exists" its facticity under the goals and ends it chooses for itself. Sartre does not deny essences to men: but he insists that all we can mean by essence is the resultant of the *pour-soi's* actions rather than any *a priori* and inescapable "human nature."

2. Continuity and stability are not denied the *pour-soi;* rather, the *pour-soi is* its memories, its past actions and choices, its physical, social, and cultural heritage in so far as it "exists" these aspects of its nature. The *pour-soi* is not an utter chaos but a dialectical continuity. The past actions, choices, attitudes, etc., of the *pour-soi* are forever in suspension in their Being; that is to say, the meaning of all of those aspects of the *pour-soi* is continually in question, since the new actions and choices of the *pour-soi* will alter or discard their importance and meaning. Although the *pour-soi* is what it is not and is not what it is, it is not an anarchic flux: its flux is dialectical. Its meaning and nature are continually being defined and redefined.

3. The meaning of choice is that the *pour-soi is* choice. It "exists" itself only by virtue of its choices. McGill has taken a typically

naturalistic definition of choice and, upon the basis of this definition, attacks Sartre's concept of choice, which is on a different level. For Sartre, choice is never completed because the *pour-soi* is in flight and continually redefines itself. We are therefore human *when* we choose. Also, for Sartre, aesthetic enjoyment, love, humor, etc., *are* aspects of the human reality and of man's freedom, since the meaning which they have for the *pour-soi* is determined only to the degree to which the *pour-soi* chooses and appropriates those aspects of its experience.

4. To be consistent with Sartre's purpose in EN, we would have to say that the "test" of freedom which McGill mentions is revealed in the ontological analysis of the *pour-soi,* because freedom exists only by virtue of the *pour-soi.* McGill desires non-ontological criteria of freedom; and with these Sartre is not concerned.

5. We must distinguish between the intuition of anguish and the psychological states which may associate themselves with the intuition of anguish. The latter, but not the former, are the proper study of the psychologists. That the psychological experiences associated with the intuition of anguish may vary, Sartre can admit without endangering his position. The *feeling* of anguish is not the unavoidable accompaniment of the human condition, since we can escape by "bad faith." Anguish as an intuitable *meaning* of the human condition is inescapable. But McGill overlooks this difference.

6. Sartre is not attempting to ignore the importance of past and present events in human experience. He is trying to show only that such events are not fatalistic constants whose meaning, once stated, is forever frozen and static. The conscious project which determines our action is itself the expression of the *pour-soi,* which *is* in so far as it is the dialectical and dynamic unity of past, present, and future.

7. This criticism ignores Sartre's description of the coefficient of adversity which faces the *pour-soi* in its existence. The slave's chains *are* an obstacle to his freedom, but the latter is meaningful only in so far as the slave wishes to be free of his manacles. In other words, it is in the project of the *pour-soi* that freedom is expressed. The chains are only an apparent obstacle to the slave's freedom because the latter *is* only in so far as the slave has chosen the end of liberty. McGill has confused the concept of liberty—physical right to go about one's business—with the ontological concept of freedom. Sartre does not argue that the slave is at liberty to scale a fifty-foot wall or to break the steel bars of his prison with his fists; he argues, rather, that the meaning

of the slavery of the individual is comprehensible only through an analysis of the situation of the *pour-soi* involved.

8. The popular appeal of a highly technical philosophic concept is no criterion for the validity of that concept. The criteria McGill wishes to set up deal with a common sense notion of freedom: one with which Sartre is not concerned here. Finally, the stipulation that man's freedom is inescapable, far from limiting the possible directives for human freedom, is the basis for asserting that such directives are unlimited. Since man is condemned to be free, everything is possible to his freedom.

Despite the answers given above to the criticisms of Mounier and McGill, we must admit that these critics of Sartre have hinted, however inadequately or mistakenly, at a certain core of truth in their analyses of freedom. This core might best be described through questions which we think Sartre fails to answer, and sometimes even fails to raise, in his ontology. These questions are: Although man "exists" his facticity, is not this facticity a sector of man's Being upon which only relative limits can be placed? Is it possible for the *pour-soi* to negate its own Nothingness via a violent flight from reality?[13] In the case of the tortured man who chooses the instant he will "give into" his torturers, the question arises: Even if we agree that he chooses his torture by relenting at a certain point, what can we say of his freedom after that point? Finally, it is necessary to ask: How will existential analysis relate ontological freedom to those areas of freedom which comprise man's social, economic, and moral values? Thus far such correlation is lacking. Sartre's short work, *Existentialism*, is but a rough and, at points, vague attempt in this direction.

2. NOTHINGNESS AND BAD FAITH

The Nothingness of the *pour-soi* consists in the fact that the *pour-soi* is what it is not and is not what it is. Consciousness is "nihilation" because it is in flight in its existence. It is perpetually remaking itself, redefining itself. The *pour-soi* is what it "is-was" (est été) in so far as its future projects reveal and interpret that "is-was"; the *pour-soi* is what it is not, because its situation is in flux. Thus, for Sartre, *Wesen ist was gewesen ist*.

---

[13] To illustrate: even if we may say that the catatonic schizophrenic chooses his disease, is there a true *pour-soi* extant *after* that choice?

The anguish of man is his awareness of his responsibility, and this responsibility is man's burden because his existence is beset by the necessity of constant choice. Since the *pour-soi* is Nothingness, it cannot appeal to any *a priori* "human nature" for guidance to action in choice. The *pour-soi is* in so far as it *is choice*. For these reasons, anguish is the stamp of man's Nothingness.

Now if man is condemned to be free as Sartre says, is there any manner in which man may choose to yield his freedom or to hide from it? In his description of *"mauvaise foi"* (bad faith), Sartre has indicated that there is a mode of Being in which the *pour-soi* seeks to "un-free" itself—to take leave of its anguish, its responsibility. Our problem, then, is to attempt to discover the relationship between Nothingness and bad faith, and to determine whether it is possible for the *pour-soi* to negate its own Nothingness and shun its responsibility.

Bad faith is the attempt of the *pour-soi* to deny itself by trying to hide from its own anguish. The *pour-soi* tries to escape its anguish by fleeing from one aspect of its nature: its "is-was." Although the *pour-soi* is not what it is, it does "exist" its "is-was" aspect (its past actions, choices, etc.). Two interpretations of this "is-was" of the *pour-soi* are possible: first, the attempt to substantialize the "is-was" into an essence. This might be illustrated by the description of man as *being* a coward because in the past he has committed certain cowardly acts. Such is the argument of those who hold for a "human nature," an essence of man which antecedes his acts and determines them. Obviously, this interpretation is the antithesis of Sartre's own position.

The second interpretation of the "is-was" is the conception of it as dialectically bound up with the existence of the *pour-soi*. The meaning of the "is-was" is continually in suspension, for man, by his actions, redefines and reinterprets his "is-was." Thus, Sartre maintains that the "is-was" of the *pour-soi* is that which the *pour-soi* is not. Now, to act in bad faith is to attempt to deny both of these interpretations.[14]

The individual who acts in bad faith seeks to negate the "is-was" of his *pour-soi*. This negation may be accomplished either by *stopping* at a certain period in one's life and refusing to take into consideration or even admit the changes that occur, or by clinging to the fact that

[14] EN, 103–104.

changes are always taking place in one's situation, and refusing to be held accountable for what one has done in the past.[15]

However, all attempts to negate the "is-was" must result in failure, because every effort to flee from anguish and responsibility inevitably takes place under an unintended but unavoidable recognition of anguish and responsibility. "The flight from anguish is only a mode of being conscious of anguish. . . . It cannot be concealed or avoided."[16] Here is the paradox of bad faith: to be in bad faith is to attempt to flee from one's anguish, but such flight is accompanied necessarily by a recognition of anguish. Sartre states the paradox in the following way: "The first act of bad faith is to flee from what one cannot flee, to flee from what one is." [17] The condition of flight from Nothingness is Nothingness; and "the condition of the possibility of dishonesty is that the human reality in its most immediate being, in the intrastructure of the pre-reflective *cogito,* must be what it is not and not be what it is." [18]

It might seem from this description that, since bad faith is a paradoxical condition, the *pour-soi* could never truly achieve the status of bad faith. To reason oneself into bad faith, to select or choose bad faith,—all such conscious actions could not lead one beyond the paradox; i.e., bad faith could not be realized, because its realization would depend on escaping from anguish, and active choice of escape from anguish means awareness of anguish. How, then, is bad faith possible?

Sartre's answer is that bad faith is not a "question of a reflected-upon and voluntary decision, but a spontaneous determination of our being." [19]

> "One is placed in bad faith as one sleeps and one is of bad faith as one dreams. Once this mode of being is realized, it is as difficult to go away from it as to wake up. Bad faith is a type of Being in the world, like insomnia or dreaming, which attempts by itself to perpetuate itself." [20]

[15] EN, 97.
[16] *Ibid.,* 82.
[17] *Ibid.,* 111.
[18] *Ibid.,* 108.
[19] *Ibid.,* 109.
[20] *Ibid.*

With this "spontaneous determination of our being" goes a weak and uncritical acceptance of the world of bad faith, an initial decision not to make decisions, an initial decision to be indecisive. Bad faith does not maintain the criteria of truth as they are accepted by the critical thought of good faith. Bad faith is resigned in advance not to be transformed into good faith.[21] Through the intitial determination of bad faith there will be obstinacy in the face of truth and a willingness to adhere to uncertain evidence.

The conclusion is that bad faith is a constant threat to consciousness: the unavoidable menace which accompanies the Nothingness of the *pour-soi*.

> "If bad faith is possible, it is because it is the immediate and permanent menace of every project of the human being, it is because consciousness conceals in its being a permanent risk of bad faith. And the origin of this risk is that consciousness, at the same time and in its being, is what it is not and is not what it is." [22]

With this exposition of bad faith in mind, we may turn to a criticism of the arguments Sartre has set forth regarding bad faith and its relationship to Nothingness.

Sartre has presented a highly ambiguous theory of bad faith. He argues, to begin with, that flight from Nothingness is *a priori* a failure, since admittance of Nothingness is presupposed in the attempted flight. Yet later he describes bad faith as a "type of being-in-the-world," and presumably this "being-in-the-world" is something more than a momentary structure. Sartre compares it to insomnia or dreaming and states that it is difficult to escape. If bad faith has this stability as a type of Being in the World, then how is it achieved? The failure to escape Nothingness would appear to render this stability inconsequential or illusory.

By holding that bad faith is not a reflective and voluntary decision "but a spontaneous determination of our being," Sartre presents a form of argument directly antithetical to what he is attempting to demonstrate. Sartre's point is that to be in bad faith is to fail to escape anguish, since choice of bad faith involves choice of anguish. Active choice is the key to the concept of bad faith. Yet when Sartre argues

---

[21] EN, 109.
[22] *Ibid.*, 111.

at the same time that active choice is not involved in the "spontaneous determination of our being," he has involved himself in a basic contradiction.

Sartre's main purpose in introducing the concept of bad faith was to show that, although man is condemned to be free, he is able to seek ways of avoiding that freedom. Bad faith is a meaningful concept only if it represents an anti-freedom value. Sartre has succeeded, however, in showing that bad faith is really only a peculiar aspect of freedom. Again, this is difficult to reconcile with the fact that he states that bad faith is the "menace" which accompanies every human project. Is the menace introduced by the *pour-soi* itself in the acts of choice of the *pour-soi* in its projects? Or is the menace of bad faith an *a priori* correlative of Nothingness which accompanies every *pour-soi*? When Sartre argues that bad faith is chosen, he is more consistent with his general position, but the meaning and force of the concept of bad faith are watered down. When Sartre argues that bad faith is some sort of spontaneous determination, he leaves the general line of his argument and make of bad faith an order of an *a priori* correlate of the *pour-soi*.

While it is clear that his general intention is to describe bad faith as the flight from anguish, from responsibility, from Nothingness, Sartre fails to make clear the nature of this flight and the import of its success or failure in its venture.

Involved in the entire concept of Nothingness and of bad faith is the problem of the facticity of the "is-was." Bad faith flees from its "is-was" because it is unwilling to accept the responsibility for the actions it has performed. But if the meaning of the acts and choices which comprise the "is-was" is always in transition, then a crucial problem arises: for what, precisely, is the *pour-soi* responsible? If I acted like a coward last year on fifteen occasions, then it would seem that these instances of cowardice comprise one sector of my "is-was." But now it is necessary to observe that these acts were acts of cowardice only in the light of certain criteria of cowardly action. Since these criteria are themselves in transition and are meaningful only in the light of my own projects, how can we say that the *pour-soi* is responsible for these cowardly acts? The meaning of cowardice is in suspension; therefore, the meaning of my past actions is also in suspension. In what sense are we responsible for them?

The point of the above criticism may be rephrased in the following way: if we are faithful to Sartre's argument, the actions which comprise the "is-was" can never be characterized as *being* acts of love, hate, violence, heroism, cowardice, deceit, etc. They may be characterized only as acts of a certain order and structure; e.g., to use love as an illustration, my "is-was" acts were acts of making certain vows, of performing certain actions, and so on, and these acts are called acts of love by definition and agreement. Thus, to be consistent, we should reduce the acts of the "is-was" to their basic structures. We cannot go beyond these basic structures and say that such and such an act *was* an act of love, because future experience may demonstrate that it was the opposite. The ardent filial love I bore my mother at the age of nine may turn out, ten years later, to have been part of an oedipus complex, which would then alter the meaning of that original love.

It is highly ambiguous to say that I am responsible for the actions of my "is-was." To follow the example just given, I am responsible for acts of kissing and hugging my mother at the age of nine, but does this mean that I am responsible for *loving* my mother at the age of nine? The latter could never be determined until the *pour-soi* is nonexistent.

The import of the criticism just made is that Sartre's concept of anguish must be extended. Since my responsibility for the acts of my "is-was" is a perpetually ambiguous one, my anguish is extended. The choices I make in the present and in the future not only define my *pour-soi* as a whole but redefine the facticity of my "is-was." By extending the concept of anguish we arrive at a more consistent interpretation of Nothingness, for it is now more clearly apparent that the *pour-soi* is that which it is not. The facticity of the *pour-soi* must be reduced to the bare structure of its past actions, whereas the *Being* of those actions is perpetually in question, because that *Being* is intimately associated with the meaning of the actions.

There is one final question concerning Sartre's conception of Nothingness: Is there any point where the human equation which is the *pour-soi* cancels out? We raised this question in the previous section by asking whether there is a true *pour-soi* extant in the catatonic schizophrenic *after* the choice of his disease (admitting the choice of the disease for the sake of the argument). Much of the criticism that has been raised against Sartre's concept of freedom is that this concept is false to reality, that it makes no sense, for example, to speak of the cremated prisoner of the concentration camp as having *freely* chosen his imprisonment and destruction. Sartre has said that either man is completely free or is not free at all. However, we may still raise the question of whether human freedom may undergo states of negation, leaving aside the question of whether those states have been initially chosen or not.

In our criticism of Sartre's theory of Nothingness and bad faith we have thus made the following points:

1. It is not clear whether bad faith is chosen by the *pour-soi* or is an *a priori* correlate of Nothingness.

2. It is unclear whether the *pour-soi* can truly achieve a status of bad faith.

3. The concept of anguish must be extended to accommodate the unsubstantiality of the "is-was."

4. It is doubtful whether there is ever a negation of the *pour-soi*.

3. BEING

In the introduction and early pages of EN, Sartre tells us that a fundamental problem he faces in his essay is to show that the two seemingly incommunicable realms of Being—the *en-soi* and the *pour-soi*—do, in fact, ultimately achieve unification in his philosophy and that he is not left with an insurmountable dualism. It will be the burden of this section of our work to attempt to prove not only that Sartre fails to resolve the dualism but also that, by his own principles, any such attempt is destined to be a failure.

Sartre attacks a series of traditional dualisms. (1) He holds that the dualism of interior-exterior of the existant is fallacious, because there is no hidden aspect of Being— no *Ding-an-sich*. He says that "the being of an existant is precisely that which it appears" to be.[23] (2) There is no dualism of appearance-essence, for appearance *is* essence (3) It is the Being of appearance which must be investigated. But upon inspection the Being of appearance reveals itself to be of two distinct varieties: the *en-soi* and the *pour-soi*. Here, then, is Sartre's problem: how can the two realms of Being be synthesized?

Sartre's first answer is the following:

"The *pour-soi* and the *en-soi* are reunited by a synthetic liaison which is no other than the *pour-soi* itself. The *pour-soi*, in effect, is nothing other than the pure nihilation of the *en-soi*; it is like a hole of being at the heart of being. . . . The *pour-soi* has no

[23] EN, 11–14.

other reality than that of being the nihilation of being. Its only qualification comes to it from the fact that it is nihilation of the individual and singular *en-soi* and not of being in general. The *pour-soi* is not nothingness in general but a singular privation; it constitutes itself as privation of *this being*." [24]

While this description answers the question, "How did the dualities arise?" or, more precisely, "How does the *pour-soi* arise?," the real question regarding the synthesis of the two polarities of Being is not answered. The solution to this problem must also be the answer to the question: *How* does the *pour-soi* unite itself with the *en-soi?* And to this question Sartre paradoxically states that an answer is not possible:

> "We do not have grounds to interrogate ourselves about the manner in which the *pour-soi* may unite itself to the *en-soi* because the *pour-soi* is in no way an autonomous substance." [25]

Were the *pour-soi* an autonomous substance, it would be what it is, but we know already that for Sartre the *pour-soi* is *not* what it is and can never be what it is—this status is reserved for the *en-soi* alone. Since the *pour-soi* is what it is not and is not what it is, it is impossible to describe the manner in which this "lack," this Nothingness, can unite itself with that which is what it is: the *en-soi*. We must conclude, therefore, that the synthetic liaison established by the *pour-soi* between the *en-soi* and the *pour-soi* is not the structure which can solve the original problem of how the two polarities of Being are synthesized. At best, the synthetic liaison is an explanatory relation which tells something about the *genesis* of the realms of Being.

But we cannot yet assert that Sartre has completely failed to solve his problem, for he makes a second attempt. He points out that prior analysis has shown that one cannot understand the *pour-soi* without immediately taking the *en-soi* into consideration, and vice versa. Unless the intimate relationship between the two realms of Being is kept in view, they are both reduced to empty abstractions:

> "The *en-soi* and the *pour-soi* are not juxtaposed. Quite to the contrary, the *pour-soi* without the *en-soi* is something like an abstraction. It could no more exist than a color without form or

[24] EN, 711–712.
[25] *Ibid.*, 712.

than a sound without highness and without timbre; a conscious-
ness which would be consciousness *of* nothing would be an
absolute nothing." [26]

Since consciousness is consciousness *of* the *en-soi*, the two are in internal
relationship which is the essence of the bond unifying *en-soi* and
pour-soi.

> "If consciousness is linked to the *en-soi* by an *internal* relation,
> does that not signify that it is articulated with it in order to con-
> stitute a totality and is it not to this totality that the name of
> *being* or of reality refers? Undoubtedly, the *pour-soi* is nihila-
> tion, but, by virtue of nihilation, it *is*; and it is in *a priori* unity
> with the *en-soi*." [27]

But, Sartre argues, even if this internal relationship does give us a
concept of Being which is a synthetic totality, we are left with the
dualism as it appears in the existant, who is still a *pour-soi* in relation
to an *en-soi*.

> "If we have to consider the total being as constituted by the
> synthetic organization of the *en-soi* and the *pour-soi,* are we not
> going to find again the difficulty which we wished to avoid? Are
> we not going to encounter again in the existant itself the hiatus
> which we discerned in the concept of being?" [28]

Sartre says that in order to be able to consider an existant as a
totality, "it is necessary that the diversity of its structures be retained
in a unitary synthesis, in such a way that each structure, envisaged
apart, is only an abstraction." [29] One part of the equation fulfills this
criterion: the *pour-soi* envisaged by itself is an abstraction. The other
half of the equation, however, does not fulfill the requirement, because
"the *en-soi* has no need of the *pour-soi* in order to be." [30] The Being
of the pure *en-soi* without consciousness is not an abstraction. Sartre
describes the way out of the difficulty in these words:

[26] EN, 715–716.
[27] *Ibid.,* 716.
[28] *Ibid.*
[29] *Ibid*
[30] *Ibid.*

"If we should wish to conceive of a synthetic organization such that the *pour-soi* is inseparable from the *en-soi* and that, reciprocally, the *en-soi* is indissolubly linked to the *pour-soi*, it would be necessary to conceive of it in such a way that the *en-soi* receives its existence from the nihilation which makes the *en-soi* take consciousness of that nihilation. What does this mean if not that the indissoluble totality of *en-soi* and *pour-soi* is conceivable only under the form of being 'cause of self.' " [31]

We may understand the nature of the form of Being which is "cause of self":

"The real is a miscarried effort to attain to the dignity of cause-of-self. Every thing happens as if the world, man, and man-in-the-world succeeded in realizing only a God who is lacking (*un Dieu manqué*). Everything happens as if the *en-soi* and the *pour-soi* were presented in a state of *disintegration* in regard to an ideal synthesis. Not that the integration has ever *taken place,* but precisely on the contrary, because it is always indicated and always impossible. It is the perpetual defeat which explains at once the indissolubility of the *en-soi* and the *pour-soi,* and their relative independence." [32]

The conclusion is that the ideal synthesis of Being is an impossible and self-contradictory structure, although if it should exist, we should know also in what manner it existed: we should know its structure.

It is disconcerting to note that if this is a correct interpretation of what Sartre is arguing, then he contradicts himself basically and has not solved his original problem. The contradiction is the following: Sartre is able to posit the possibility of an ideal synthesis of Being by a "pre-ontological comprehension of the self-caused being."[33] The comprehension is *pre*-ontological because it is of an *ideal* and not a real structure. Ontological analysis can be made of *real* (i.e., existant) structures only. Yet Sartre states that ontological analysis *includes* analysis of the region of "cause of self." He writes: "For ontology, the only regions of being which can be elucidated are those of the *en-soi,* the *pour-soi,* and the ideal region of the 'cause of self'."[34] Apart from the fact that ontology cannot analyze *ideal* regions, it remains a con-

[31] EN, 716–717.
[32] *Ibid.,* 717.
[33] *Ibid.*
[34] *Ibid.,* 719.

tradiction to hold, in view of what Sartre said earlier, that the ideal region of "cause of self" can be comprehended both pre-ontologically and ontologically.

Thus, in his analysis of "cause of self," Sartre has not solved his original problem of the synthesis of the polarities of Being. If "the real is a miscarried effort to attain to the dignity of cause-of-self," if "everything happens . . . as if the *en-soi* and the *pour-soi* were presented in a state of *disintegration*," then it must follow that the ultimate integration of *en-soi* and *pour-soi* must remain an incomplete and unrealizable ideal. The dualism is *not* resolved, and the two realms of Being find no true integration. Surprisingly, this is what Sartre himself points out when he says that the integration of *en-soi* and *pour-soi* is "always impossible." [35]

Sartre's conclusion to the argument concerning the resolution of the dualism of Being is this: "If it is impossible to pass from the notion of being-*en-soi* to that of being-*pour-soi* and to reunite them in a common genre, then the *passage in fact* from one to the other and their reunion cannot be brought about." [36] But it is not possible to reconcile this statement with his earlier claim that his analysis of Being will not end in a dualism of two incommunicable realms of Being.

The only consistent conclusion that may be drawn from Sartre's ontological analysis of Being is the one which he hints at in certain places but does not make explicit, and which he later contradicts. The logical conclusion of his argument is that a self-caused Being "is *impossible* and that its concept . . . contains a contradiction." [37] The contradiction is that man is the creature who aspires to be the *en-soi-pour-soi*. This aspiration must end in failure in principle, for the *pour-soi* cannot be its own proper foundation, since it is what it is not—since it is Nothingness.

A further aspect of the logical conclusion to Sartre's problem is that if the ideal *whole* can be imagined or posited, it is *only* imaginable or positable—never realizable. This is the paradox of the *en-soi-pour-soi*. The paradox of Being, therefore, is Sartre's proper conclusion. However, if this conclusion is accepted, Sartre must give up the claims made in his introduction to EN, in which he berated the traditional philosophic positions for their unsolvable dualisms.

[35] EN, 717.
[36] *Ibid.*
[37] *Ibid.*

The logical conclusion to Sartre's own ontology is an unbridgeable dualism. Only within this dualism can all the structures of Being which Sartre describes retain their meaning and consistency. The crucial relations of freedom, choice, situation, etc., all receive consistent interpretation if we understand Sartre's concept of Being as essentiallly dualistic. The relation of freedom may serve as an example of what is intended here.

The *pour-soi* is free because it exists as "lack"; i.e., it has no stable or permanent structure which it *is*. Rather, the *pour-soi* must continually define and redefine itself. It must *make* itself as it goes along. Now, the *pour-soi* is free because it is not the foundation of its Being. Were it *en-soi-pour-soi*, it would be a permanent and substantial structure: it would be God. However, if we assume now that the *pour-soi* and the *en-soi* are united in such a manner that the *pour-soi* causes the *en-soi* to be, then the concept of the freedom of the *pour-soi* is distorted, and the *pour-soi* itself no longer exists in the way Sartre has previously described. The same applies to the concepts of choice and situation, because they, too, are profoundly bound up with the structure of the *pour-soi*.

If his ontology were revised so that the *en-soi* and the *pour-soi* were made attributes of Being after the fashion of Spinoza, then every structure of Being Sartre has described would lose its unique meaning and he would have accomplished no more than a reformulation of traditional ontologies. The validity, consistency, and significance of Sartre's ontology require the unresolvable dualism of *en-soi* and *pour-soi*.

Chapter VIII

SARTRE'S "COPERNICAN REVOLUTION":
AN INTERPRETATION

Sartre's "Copernican revolution" is essentially the attempt to formulate at the ontological level what Kant attempted to show at the epistemological level: that the phenomenal world we experience is the resultant of the activity of the forms of cognition upon a primordial "given." The basic similarity between Sartre and Kant which must be kept in mind is that for Sartre the 'molding' of phenomenal reality is at the ontological level derivative of and dependent upon the activity of the *pour-soi,* which both "exists" reality and exists *in* reality. There are important dissimilarities, however, between the two Copernican revolutions. Kant describes the action of the forms of sensibility and of cognition which ultimately constitute the synthetic unity identified as the phenomenal object. Sartre, on the other hand, is not concerned with deducing the categories or determining how synthetic *a priori* propositions are possible and valid for experience; rather, he wishes to find out in what way the human reality is a function of two polarities: the *en-soi* and the *pour-soi.* By introducing his Copernican revolution and asserting the priority of the *pour-soi,* Sartre attempts to demonstrate how the dialectic of relationships which hold between the *en-soi* and the *pour-soi* is ultimately comprehensible. It should be added, of course, that Sartre nowhere uses the term "Copernican revolution" to describe this approach to Being; it is implicit rather than explicit in his writing. What follows here is, therefore, an interpretation and not an exposition of what Sartre himself has said.

In our expository section we stressed the fact that there is a strong realistic element in Sartre. The *pour-soi* "exists" its reality, but also it exists *in* its reality. By this we understand the following: to "exist" reality is to constitute the reality about us—to appropriate the object. To exist *in* reality is to be a *pour-soi* among other *pour-sois* in a world whose significations are not all *my* significations but contain the significations of Others; it is to admit the objective existence of the object through the idea of the coefficient of adversity. For Sartre, reality is the complex: "existed" and existed-*in*. The polarities of Being *are* reality, i.e., that which is "existed" is the function of the *pour-soi*, and that which exists *in* is the function of the *en-soi*. But at this point a crucial difficulty arises.

It is one thing to assert that the *meaning* of experience is dependent on the meaning-giver: the *pour-soi*; it is quite another thing to hold that the object itself is constituted by the *pour-soi*. The Kantian Copernican revolution can be interpreted in two ways: either as a working hypothesis in the attempt to explicate the knowing process, or as a metaphysical interpretation which holds that the constitution of the object is directly dependent upon the categories of the understanding in such a manner that, without the synthetic operation of the categories, the constituted object would be impossible and there would be no phenomenal reality. It is here that we find the variation in the interpretation of Kant: the realistic interpretation which considers the activity of mind in the knowing process as fulfilling a strictly logical role of synthesis of meaning, and the subjectivistic interpretation which holds that the phenomenal object is the resultant of the activity of mind as it molds or shapes what is given to it.

Should Sartre's Copernican revolution be given a realistic or a subjectivistic interpretation? Under the headings of signification by Others, coefficient of adversity, etc., we have already dealt with the realistic basis in Sartre's philosophy. We cannot accept the realistic interpretation completely because of contrary evidence: Sartre's intense stress on the appropriative techniques of the *pour-soi*. Sartre has told us that "the known object is my thought as thing" [1] and that "to have is to *create*" [2] and that "the original and radical rapport of creation is a rapport of emanation. . . . That which I create . . . is myself . . . To the degree to which I appear to myself as *creating* the objects by the sole rapport of *appropriation*, these objects are *me*." [3] Sartre repeatedly stresses the importance of both subjectivist and objectivist approaches. Phenomenological ontology is to cut across the positions of both idealism and realism.

---

[1] EN, 668.
[2] *Ibid.*, 680.
[3] *Ibid.*, 680–681.

Complete appropriation is an ideal and not a realizable structure of experience. "It is impossible to realize the relation symbolized by appropriation," [4] since realization would mean an impossible synthesis—the synthesis, namely, of the *en-soi-pour-soi*. If, as Sartre maintains, appropriation is a symbolic relation, then any true Copernican revolution in the metaphysical sense is ruled out. Sartre, however, has not accepted a strictly non-metaphysiacl interpretation.

Whether we accept a subjectivist or realist interpretation of Kant, it is still true that for him the sensibility and the understanding are stable structures. As necessary preconditions of the possibility of experience they are constants. If they did change somehow, the experience we might imagine ourselves to have would not be what we could understand as human experience. For Sartre, however, such constant and unchanging categories cannot be introduced into the nature of the *pour-soi*, for the latter is that which it is not and is not that which it is. The *pour-soi*, then, is in a constant state of unfulfillment—in a state of "lack." At the ontological level no categorial constants can be ascribed to it. Hence, if the *pour-soi* molds experience or legislates the nature of its situation, that molding or legislation takes place within a framework of flux and transition of meanings. But if now the nature of the *pour-soi* is such that a hypothetical interpretation of the Copernican revolution is ruled out (since appropriation is a projective but unaccomplished relation), what is left?

Sartre's Copernican revolution at the ontological level places the *pour-soi* at the core of existence. The *pour-soi* has priority because it *is* its situation. However, since the *pour-soi* is in perpetual flux, the significations which it creates change with it. In short, the constancy or regularity of the phenomenal world of Kant has been denied, and in its place is put a dialectical reality. The essence of Sartre's Copernican revolution, therefore, is that the manifestation of the *pour-soi* is dialectical reality. Reality exists through situation, and situation is a function of the *pour-soi*. To be sure, the *en-soi* does have a facticity which is independent of and prior to the individual *pour-soi*, but the meaning of the *en-soi* is determinable only through the *pour-soi*. Thus, Sartre's Copernican revolution establishes two points: 1) that reality is a function of the *pour-soi* although it is not the phenomenal world of Kant; it is the dialectical reality which the *pour-soi* "exists";

[4] EN, 683.

2) that the facticity of things has realistic status, but that the meaning of this status depends on the interpretation it receives from the *pour-soi*. In a certain sense, therefore, the Copernican revolution intended by Sartre has never been and never can be completed. It is a perpetual and on-going process. Its meaning is continually in suspension.

Is it of value to introduce this interpretation of the Copernican revolution into Sartre's work? We said earlier that Sartre has performed his revolution on the ontological rather than the epistemological plane. His revolution gives an explanation of how Being is determined by human Being, or, to put it in another way, how the *en-soi* is determined by the *pour-soi*. But if our interpretation of Sartre's Copernican revolution is correct, the resultant of the revolution is a non-stable reality, is Being in flux. The importance of having introduced the concept of the Copernican revolution into this discussion lies in the fact that we may now use it as an interpretive category in furthering our understanding of Sartre's ontology, in particular, the nature of appropriation.

The appropriative relation is, in principle, incomplete and must, therefore, remain an ideal. Appropriation for the *pour-soi* is appropriation only of certain segments of the objects of experience, of those segments, namely, which the *pour-soi* holds in its situation. The *en-soi* of some unchartered peak in the Himalayan Mountains is not "existed" by me. I do not appropriate it; it is not I. However, the mountain I climb with great difficulty *is* I. I appropriate it in conquering it.

> "The totality of my possessions reflects the totality of my being. I *am* what I *have*. *It is I* that I touch on this cup, on this trinket. This mountain which I climb, *it is I* to the degree to which I conquer it; and when I am at its summit, which I have 'acquired' at the price of some efforts, I *am* this large view over the valley and the surrounding mountains; the panorama is I expanded to the horizon, for its exists only because of me and for me." [5]

And further:

> "Possession is a magic rapport. I *am* these objects which I possess, but outside of me. That which I posses is me outside of

[5] EN, 680–681.

me, outside of all subjectivity as an *en-soi* which escapes me at each instant and whose creation I perpetuate at each instant." [6]

The conquered mountain is I as *en-soi*. But this *en-soi* is, as it were, an externalized internality—a projection of my *pour-soi* which has momentarily become *en-soi*. This *en-soi* is impermanent. It has no stability of its own, it fades. It necessitates constant renewing for survival and is a "creation I perpetuate at each instant." Such *en-soi* is impermanent, because the *pour-soi* is organically incapable of founding its own Being.

Thus, Sartre has shown that the *pour-soi* can create a certain type of *en-soi*, but that such *en-soi* is impermanent because its existence is constantly in suspension; it is like a paralytic who depends upon a machine to keep him breathing and whose life would be terminated the moment the machine stopped working. It seems, then, that the one form of the true metaphysical creation of which the *pour-soi* is capable is, in principle, doomed to failure. Upon ascending the mountain, *I* am the mountain, but the *en-soi* which is the I that is the mountain is an *en-soi* that can never be realized in true permanence and stability.

Making use of the Copernican revolution as an interpretive category, we may attempt one more and final analysis of a certain existential problem: Sartre's idea of situation. The *pour-soi*, in order to be *pour-soi*, must be engaged. It must choose itself in a situation. The *pour-soi* "exists" the situation. All of the significations, the meanings of projects, the interpretation of rapports, the grasping of the facticity of objects, and so on—all of these, making up the reality of the *pour-soi*, are the *pour-soi* and define its existence. Now, if we admit that through the thesis of the Copernican revolution the *pour-soi* constitutes its dialectical reality ("exists" its situation), then it must follow that the *pour-soi* is responsible for its situation. Further, since the situation of the *pour-soi* includes other *pour-sois*, it also follows that the *pour-soi* is responsible for Others as well. If, as Sartre says, situation is possible only through choices of the *pour-soi*, then these choices involve a grave responsibility, for they affect completely and profoundly the status of Others. In *Existentialism* we learn that, when we choose, we choose all mankind and involve thereby all mankind. Thus we choose in anguish.

[6] EN, 681.

Since Sartre has not pursued the value question in EN, it is unnecessary for us to continue further with this analysis. We see, however, that, as an interpretive category, the thesis of Sartre's Copernican revolution goes far toward explaining many aspects of his philosophy which otherwise would remain unconnected or obscure. For example, the frequently recurring statement that Being *haunts* the *pour-soi* now becomes intelligible. The *pour-soi* is haunted by the *en-soi* which it can never absorb or with which it can never become one; it is haunted by its passion to make itself the Absolute: God. It is haunted also by the fact that, while it "exists" its reality, it can never stabilize that reality; it must re-create it at every moment. The responsibility for this re-creation is the anguish of the *pour-soi*. It is anguish that haunts the *pour-soi,* the anguish of *Being.*

Chapter IX

FINAL EVALUATION

"Metaphysics is not a sterile discussion about abstract notions which have nothing to do with experience. It is a living effort to embrace from within the human condition in its totality."

—Sartre

In our introduction we described the general area of existential thought, both literary and philosophic, and we attempted to show in this connection that Sartre's technical philosophy cannot be understood from his popular novels or plays or public lectures, but that he is a serious philosopher attempting to investigate the problem of Being via a phenomenological ontology, and that it is only by an examination of his EN that a real comprehension of his philosophic thought can be attained. We indicated further that certain fundamental questions face Sartre's projected ontology: Does phenomenology have the inner capacity to expand into a critical theory of knowledge and into an ontology? Is phenomenology a generalized Kantianism? And, finally, in what sense is Sartre's variety of phenomenology indebted to Husserl and Hegel? We shall return to these questions in order to indicate our final conclusions regarding Sartre's answers to them.

After an exposition of the structure and content of EN, we turned to our criticisms of the work. In the discussion of phenomenological method we described Husserl's phenomenology and attempted to show that Sartre's method is distinctly non-Husserlian and that the only valid sense in which it can be termed "phenomenological" is in the Hegelian sense of the term. In this respect EN is in many ways a restatement of the *Phenomenology of Mind*. The significance of Sartre's failure to adopt Husserl's method we shall discuss later.

Next, we examined three central theses of EN: Freedom, Nothingness and Bad Faith, and Being. In the first thesis, we examined the Sartrean concept of freedom and defended it against the attacks of several critics who, we claimed, had misinterpreted its meaning. We reserved our own criticisms of Sartre's doctrine of freedom for the second thesis on Nothingness and Bad Faith, because this thesis is intimately tied to the concept of freedom. Our major point of criticism of Sartre's concept of Nothingness was that the idea of human responsibility, which is the core of the concept of Nothingness, is presented in a paradoxical light: it is not clear from the discussions in EN whether Bad Faith (flight from responsibility) is a "possible" of the *pour-soi*. Associated with this criticism is our discovery of the uncertain status of the facticity (the "is-was") of the *pour-soi* and the role it plays in human freedom.

In the third thesis on Being we investigated the fundamental dualism of the *en-soi* and the *pour-soi* in Sartre's ontology. After showing that the essence of Sartre's contribution to ontology lies in the *a priori* incapacity of the *pour-soi* to become its own foundation: to become *en-soi-pour-soi* (the Absolute or God), we demonstrated that Sartre's attempt to resolve the dualism through some sort of synthetic liaison or idea of "detotalized totality" must prove a failure for two main reasons: first, because the structure of the argument in EN requires the dualism, and, second, because the *ideal* synthesis of the polarities of Being would transcend the reach of ontological analysis.

The final critical section is concerned with what we have termed Sartre's Copernican revolution. The criticism raised there is that in Sartre's description of the dialectic of relationships which holds between the *en-soi* and the *pour-soi*, there is contained implicitly an attempt to formulate at the ontological level something analagous to Kant's revolution in epistemology. Rather than its being introduced as a working hypothesis, Sartre's revolution, we held, is the outcome of his kind of phenomenological inspection of what is given in experience. The importance of raising the question of an ontological revolution is that, having formulated the idea of a Copernican revolution, we may then use it as an interpretive category in the analysis of other areas in Sartre's thought which might otherwise remain obscure. Thus, via the Copernican revolution, we re-examined such vital Sartrean concepts as "appropriation" and "situation" and were able to secure a more complete understanding of Sartre. Finally, we showed that through clarification of the concepts of appropriation and situation, we were able to achieve greater insight into his doctrine of human responsibility: the profound relationship between the *pour-soi*, human freedom, human responsibility, and existential anguish.

With this summary of our work in mind, we turn now to questions raised in the introduction.

(1) Does phenomenology have the inner capacity to expand into a critical theory of knowledge and into an ontology? Despite the fact that writers such as Farber have attempted to present Husserl's phenomenology as strictly philosophic method, it nevertheless remains true that Husserl himself, in later years, developed a position in many respects close to the transcendental idealism of the Kantians. In accepting Husserl's method in the extremely limited and partial sense we have previously indicated, Sartre cannot be said to be part of the movement of the followers of Husserl, who are attempting to carry his work forward in various special fields. It is not, therefore, Sartre's intention to attempt the expansion of Husserl's phenomenology into an ontology. We shall return later to the question of whether or not such an expansion is possible.

(2) Is phenomenology a generalized Kantianism? This question remains a general problem confronting Husserlian phenomenology rather than a specific question for Sartre. We have tried to show in the section on Sartre's Copernican revolution that on the ontological level, he faces some questions basically similar to the questions Kant faced. The answer to the question of whether phenomenology is a generalized Kantianism should come from Husserl rather than from Sartre.

Perhaps the basic similarity between Husserl and Kant is that both are profoundly concerned with a non-psychological exploration of the categorial structure and content of subjectivity in general and of consciousness in particular. As for Kant the problem of knowledge is referred back to cognition and is analyzed there transcendentally, so for Husserl "Phenomenology refers the being of the world back to the transcendental subjectivity in whose life the world is 'valid'." [1] One way of referring to Husserl's concern with subjectivity is to view it in the light of the Kantian problem of the a priori. Thus, according to Farber, "Husserl has formulated the method which is implicit in all attempts, from Kant to Lewis, to determine the a priori aspect of experience." [2] What is pursued by Husserl is the typically Kantian

---

[1] Farber, M., *The Foundation of Phenomenology*, 553.
[2] *Ibid.*, 562.

quest for that comprehension obtainable "only by an analysis which gives an account of the part played by mind (or subjectivity) in its relationship with that which is 'given' in experience." [3]

Although we can give no final answer to Husserl's own ideas regarding the inner capacity of phenomenology to be expanded into a generalized Kantianism, we do know that phenomenology deals with basically Kantian questions, that Husserl, in his later philosophizing, turned more and more to a sympathetic interpretation of Kant and, finally, that some of his writings indicate that, had he lived to complete his projected work, he would have taken up many of the questions we have considered in the course of this work, and especially the basic questions we have now raised regarding the relationships between phenomenology, Kantianism, and ontology. The demonstration of Husserl's concern with these areas is revealed convincingly when Farber writes:

> "It was Husserl's aim through the years to determine the genuine concept of the analytic, as distinguished from Kant's unclear concept of it, and to distinguish the genuine analytic ontology from the essentially different material (synthetic-*a priori*) ontology. After the appearance of the *Logical Investigations* he planned a systematic theory of categories, or of the possible regions of being; and he was careful to distinguish the phenomenological *a priori* from the ontological *a priori*." [4]

We might conclude our answer to the question of the relationship between Husserl's phenomenology and Kantianism by pointing out that there was an agreeable and close kinship between the Marburg school of Neo-Kantianism and Husserl's phenomenology. In the opinion of Husserl, Natorp was one of the very few critics who understood his work as it appeared in *Logical Investigations*. This thread of communal interest and mutual respect which runs through the relationship of phenomenology and Neo-Kantianism continues to the present day. [5]

---

[3] Farber, M., *The Foundation of Phenomenology*, 562.

[4] *Ibid.*, 206.

[5] It can be observed in the interest of Cassirer in phenomenology and in the interest of such representatives of the phenomenological school as Fritz Kaufman in Neo-Kantianism. The intended "dialogue" between Cassirer and Kaufman which was to take up these very problems was made impossible by the death of Cassirer. See Kaufman, F., "Neo-Kantianism and Phenomenlogy."

(3) In what sense is Sartre's variety of phenomenology indebted to Husserl and Hegel? We have largely answered this question in our section on phenomenological method by showing in detail what the Husserlian method of phenomenology is and how Sartre departs radically from it. We concluded in that section that the only true sense in which Sartre can call his ontology "phenomenological" is the Hegelian sense of that term. Accordingly we wrote that EN is in large part a restatement of Hegel's *Phenomenology of Mind*. But the real question that arises in this connection is: What is the significance of Sartre's abandonment of Husserlian phenomenological method? What effect does this abandonment have on his ontological inquiry?

In the final analysis, Sartres "radical' ontology rests upon the claim to a new method of dealing with the questions of ontology. Unless he does use a new method, his work can be considered only as a repetition of the old. If we realize that it has been the burden of much contemporary philosophy—the positivistic movement, in particular—to rid philosophy of the traditional morasses and forests of empty verbiage which have resulted from metaphysical systems, it would be only a poor excuse for Sartre's claim to originality to have merely restated Hegelian philosophy.

From the very start of EN, Sartre attacks prior ontologies and philosophic positions as having led to unresolvable dualisms and impasses; phenomenological ontology is created for the very purpose of overcoming the difficulties of this situation. Thus, Sartre's work, judged by his own claims and intentions, can be considered a meaningfully new approach to ancient problems only if his method is new and distinctive. He leads us to believe that it is Husserl's method he will employ, but then proceeds to abandon that method and, without overt statement, returns to Hegelian phenomenology. Because of this abandonment, he gives up the one hope he offered for precise and clear methodology. Let us see if we can get to the heart of Sartre's reason for departing from Husserlian method.

In accepting Husserl's idea that all consciousness is consciousness *of* something, Sartre places his ontology on the terrain of Husserl's starting point: subjectivity. With Husserl, Sartre agrees that the Cartesian point of orientation is the only true starting point in philosophic inquiry. However, where Husserl develops strict methods for the inspection of intentionality, Sartre does not. In giving up the theory of intentionality, Sartre departs drastically from Husserlian phenomenology. His quarrel with Husserlian intentionality is, fundamentally, that it results in that variety of idealism which fails to found transcendent Being.

> "During his whole philosophical career, Husserl was haunted by the idea of transcendance and passing-beyond. But the philosophic instruments which he used, in particular his idealist conception of existence, deprived him of this transcendance. His intentionality is only the carricature of it. The Husserlian consciousness can, in reality, transcend itself neither toward the world nor toward the future, nor toward the past." [6]

The difficulty in understanding Sartre's use of phenomenology arises because he does not completely give up the Husserlian phenomenology. He retains its starting point in intentionality, but this retention of the starting point is not a retention of the meaning, nature, or use of Husserlian intentionality. All of these are given up. What does Sartre put in their place?

We observed in an earlier section that Sartre makes considerable use of a kind of "ontological argument." It is his use of the ontological form of arguing that replaces the distinctive method of intentionality as developed by Husserl. Sartre's ontological proof of transphenomenal Being begins with the idea of intentionality, with the idea, that is, that consciousness is consciousness *of* something. However, he does not continue the argument as the tradition of Anselm would have it, i.e., he does not argue that there must be Being because we have an idea of it. Rather, Sartre argues that subjectivity itself is possible only on the condition that what it is conscious *of* is a real and transphenomenal existant. Consciousness of Being, he contends, is a revealing intuition which implies a revealed.[7] Thus, "to say that consciousness is consciousness *of* something, is to say that it must be produced as revelation-revealed of a being which is not it and which is given as existant already at the time it reveals it." [8] Sartre concludes that "there is an ontological proof valid for the whole domain of consciousness." [9]

The "revealing" of Being returns us to our earlier criticism in the section on phenomenological method in which we stated that the concept of proof or demonstration in Sartre resolves itself into an

[6] EN, 152–153.
[7] *Ibid.*, 28–29.
[8] *Ibid.*
[9] *Ibid.*, 30.

order of "revealing" of the status of ontological affairs. It is now possible to see that the ontological proof is not a proof in the traditional scholastic sense but an ontologically "revealed" condition of Being.

What has Sartre gained and lost by this substitution of ontological proof for Husserlian method? According to his own views, he has gained that transcendance of Being which, he claims, "haunted" Husserl's philosophizing; unfortunately, he has gained it (granting, at present and for the sake of the argument, its validity) at the cost of replacing any rationally comprehensible form of proof with a psychological, nearly-mystical, and ontic sort of demonstrability. This form of demonstration is quasi-phenomenological in so far as it stems from the Husserlian theory of intentionality, but it is non-phenomenological in so far as it takes advantage of the "natural attitude" as its principle of verification.

This Sartean method is consistently used only in the opening pages of EN. After Sartre, admittedly, fails to accomplish an ontological proof for the existence of the Other, he uses the phenomenological method sporadically and inconsistently. Throughout the sections on the concrete relations between selves, he leaves all forms or degrees of phenomenology and gives us a psychologistic account of sadism, masochism, sexuality, etc. In existential psychoanalysis he abandons phenomenological philosophizing. Only in the last third of EN, when he returns to the problem of human freedom, does he seek to reestablish his phenomenological lines; but by this time his analyses are largely based on what has gone before, and this prior content, to a great degree, reduces his analysis to existential psychoanalysis. Now, for Sartre, existential psychoanalysis is valid because it rests upon previously established ontological foundations, but since those supposed ontological foundations are shot through with psychologism, as well as with genuine intuitions and keen insights—none of which being the instruments Sartre purports to be using—the arguments based upon these foundations cannot be validated, not even on Sartre's own grounds.

Summarizing our criticism of Sartre's method, we may therefore say that, through the abandonment of true Husserlian phenomenology, Sartre invalidates his inquiry and the resultant ontology, because of the lack of a clear and consistent method. Sartre is drawn from ontological to psychological analysis and thus fails to present a clear theory of proof. Without such a theory of proof Sartre's ontology is left wide open to the attacks of positivism: the general charge being that Sartrean terminology is meaningless and Sartre's problem a "pseudo-problem." The nerve of the positivist attack lies in the claim that the propositions of ontology—as of metaphysics—are nonsensical and that, accordingly, the time has come to purge contemporary philosophizing of such meaningless and useless hindrances to clear thinking.

Ayer gives a concise statement of the positivistic rejection of metaphysics when he writes:

> "We may . . . define a metaphysical sentence as a sentence which purports to express a genuine proposition, but does, in fact, express neither a tautology nor an empirical hypothesis. And as tautologies and empirical hypotheses form the entire class of significant propositions, we are justified in concluding that all metaphysical assertions are nonsensical." [10]

With metaphysics eliminated, the concept of philosophy which remains is described as follows:

> "The propositions of philosophy are not factual, but linguistic in character—that is, they do not describe the behavior of physical, or even mental, objects; they express definitions, or the formal consequences of definitions. Accordingly, we may say that philosophy is a department of logic." [11]

In a recent work on analytic philosophy, Arthur Pap tells us that "a metaphysical statement is not just at the time unverified but unverifiable in principle." [12] Also, "according to positivist usage . . . a metaphysical statement is one which it is *logically* impossible to verify." [13] Examples of metaphysical statements for positivist writers are: "There was a time when matter was created" and "There is a cause which itself is uncaused, that is, a first mover." [14] It is obvious to any reader of EN that the complex, often obscure, figurative, and elusive language of Sartre yields statements which are much worse instances of what the positivists term "nonsense." It is enough to call to mind such a key statement as Sartre's characterization of the *pour-*

[10] Ayer, A. J., *Language, Truth and Logic,* 41.
[11] *Ibid.,* 57.
[12] Pap, A., *Elements of Analytic Philosophy,* 9.
[13] *Ibid.,* 10.
[14] *Ibid.,* 12.

soi (as that which is what it is not and is not what it is) in order to realize that positivists would term the great majority of sentences in EN nonsensical. And this, in fact, is the case in Ayer's review of EN. He berates "the attempt to endow Nothing with an activity, the fruit of which is found in such statements as Heidegger's *'das Nichts nichtet'* or Sartre's *'le Néant est néantisé'* "[15] "Whatever may be the effective value of these statements," Ayer writes, "I cannot but think that they are literally nonsensical." [16] His conclusion is: "What is called existentialist philosophy has become very largely an exercise in the art of misusing the verb 'to be'." [17]

How can Sartre meet such criticism? Can EN be justified as philosophy after the onslaught of positivism? In defense of Sartre one might attempt the following replies to the general positivistic criticism. First, the analysis of Being is prior to any epistemological considerations. Whereas the positivist wishes to set up criteria for verifiability of propositions, the ontologist is interested in analyzing the primal given from which all analyses ultimately derive. The epistemologist assumes the Being of his area of investigation in the sense that any attempt to define Being via logical constructs removes the investigation one step from the "originary givens" of our experience and so departs from pure Being.

Second, Sartre might claim that his "phenomenological" method offers the possibility of verifying the propositions concerning Being and Nothingness which he formulates. In some sense, this method does center about the formulation of arguments on the basis of individual and direct insights into and inspections of the given. The idea that truths regarding the given will be revealed to the phenomenologist is then a basic departure from the main line of contemporary philosophic analysis. This departure is what makes Sartre's, at least in part, a "radical" ontology. Since the positivist rules out by definition verification through "revelation," he can never hope to comprehend Sartre's method or results.

Third, the difficulty which the positivist has in understanding Sartre's work is one partially of philosophic orientation, temperament, and sympathy. Although in the course of this work we have not

---

[15] Ayer, A. J., "Novelist-philosophers, V, Jean-Paul Sartre," *Horizon*, July, Vol. XII, No. 67, 1945, 16.

[16] *Ibid.*, 19.

[17] *Ibid.*, 25.

stressed the "irrational" aspect of Sartre's philosophy, it must be recalled that existential philosophy has such a quality.[18] We understand the irrationalism of EN when we realize that the *pour-soi* is Nothingness and that, as Nothingness, it cannot support itself with the traditional categories of thought. Sartre, therefore, forsakes all theories which hold for an essence of man, and brings forth instead his categories of anguish and nihilation. Sartre's countercharge against the positivists might be that they are a part of the tradition of philosophy which clings to the rationalist categories and which holds for an essence of man—a human nature. The implicit presupposition of thinkers like Ayer is that the world is of such a nature that logical analysis may reveal its structure. But Sartre might argue that without ontological analysis such a position is unwarranted.

Fourth, the considerations stated above regarding the radical categoriology of existentialism lead to an important difference between Sartrean and positivistic analysis. The existentialist claims that he is exploring areas of human reality which are closed to positivistic approaches. It is certainly clear that, apart from the validity of Sartre's work, he *has* attempted to analyze the concepts of human freedom, choice, and so on. Positivists have excluded such concepts from their work for various reasons: that they are the proper object of study for different disciplines— psychology or social theory; that empirical verification of propositions concerning human freedom (in the way that Sartre deals with the problem) is impossible in principle. Sartre, however, might answer these arguments by asserting that the ontological investigation of man's "situation" cannot be the work of special disciplines, because they all begin by presupposing the very object of ontological inquiry: the Being of man. Further, existentialism is reacting against the system of traditional and fixed categories of the special sciences. Man's existential fear, dread, suffering, aloneness, and anguish are incomprehensible when viewed as psychological or psychiatric disturbances to be cured by proper clinical therapy. Similarly, the existential category of responsibility of the *pour-soi* is meaningless if it is understood in terms of the "responsibility" of the business executive, the civic "responsibility" of the citizen, or the religious "responsibility" of the Christian. The positivists, on the other hand, deny validity to the existential area of inquiry *by fiat*: they assert that

---

[18] See Introduction.

all areas not the objects of positivistic inquiry are necessarily referred to the special sciences.

Fifth, Sartre may claim that his ontology is in the tradition of "perennial philosophy." This statement is more than an argument *ad vericundum*. Jaspers writes of the spirit of perennial philosophy:

> "Today as at all times we must do the work of the philosophical craft: develop the categories and methods that constitute the structure of our basic knowledge, orient ourselves in the cosmos of the sciences, assimilate the history of philosophy, practice speculative thinking in metaphysics, and apply the elucidating methods of existential philosophy.
>
> The aim of philosophy is at all times to achieve the *independence* of man as an individual. This he gains by establishing a relation to authentic being. He gains independence of everything that happens in the world by the depth of his attachment to transcendance. What Lao Tse found in the Tao, Socrates in the divine mission and in knowledge, Jeremiah in Yahweh who revealed himself to him, what Boethius, Bruno, Spinoza knew: that was what made them independent." [19]

Perennial philosophy has as its quest what Plato called "the healing of our unwisdom." But, more precisely, the meaning of perennial philosophy centers about a rich appreciation of the great questions and answers of the history of philosophy, and is a passionate concern with the problems raised by the dominant figures of philosophic inquiry. We must be careful to state here that agreement with the core of perennial philosophy does not compel the contemporary thinker to accept any special philosophic position nor to hold that *every* utterance ever made by an important philosopher is in some degree true. Rather, perennial philosophy is desirous of keeping intact the dialectic of history of philosophy so that what has been gained in insight over the past centuries will not be either overlooked or purposely ignored in the rush of certain contemporary thinkers to ostracize from philosophy everything which dates earlier than the work of Frege. It is agreed that the idea of perennial philosophy is a "loose" and undemanding one, but its importance is to be observed, ironically, more in those who revolt against it with a great show of indignation than in those who accept it as a worthy guide and a meaningful directive.

[19] Jaspers, K., *The Perennial Scope of Philosophy*, 166.

Sartre's place in perennial philosophy is assured in the sense that he raises again the great metaphysical question of Being. Thus, he is in that line of philosophizing which begins with Aristotle and contains in its ranks the names of Aquinas, Spinoza, Leibnitz, Descartes, Kant, Hegel, Husserl, and Heidegger. The "unwisdom" of many of the positivists lies in their rejecting, by *ex cathedra* pronouncement, this history of problems related to theory of Being, basing their action on the assertion that the problem of Being is unresolvable. The advice of perennial philosophy is that "unresolvable" problems are no less the province of philosophic study than are "resolvable" ones, and that the worth of philosophy lies as much in questions that are raised as in the solutions to those questions, as much in clarifying the "unresolvable" as in solving the resolvable. "Science and philosophy," Santayana writes, "cast a net of words into the sea of being, happy in the end if they draw anything out besides the net itself, with some holes in it."

Last, in responding with Sartre to the accusations of positivism, we must be careful to admit some of the *similarities* between these seemingly completely contradictory and disparate positions. The basic similarity we shall stress is one of historical genesis. Both positions are seriously concerned with the Cartesian-Husserlian problem of the proper starting point in philosophizing. Both positions are in some sense thrown back upon the *cogito* as the only certain point of orientation. Both positions are in approximate agreement in the usage of methodological solipsism as the key to correct philosophical procedure. Sartre might claim that from this point on the dissimilarities multiply because ontology analyzes the primordial level of the human reality and positivism goes 'forward' to the analysis of language, formal methods, and the complexus of problems associated with these. Whereas Sartre desires a phenomenological explication of the subject-pole of experience, positivism turns to an analysis of the object-pole by use of hypothetico-deductive methods. These comparisons must not be misconstrued to imply that Sartrean existentialism and modern positivism are basically alike or that they may be synthesized: such an assertion would be completely false. We have attempted only to point out, in the vast welter of obvious differences between the two positions, a basic similarity which derives from the historico-genetic aspects of both existentialism and positivism.

It must be remembered that, for the main part, the above replies to positivistic criticisms of Sartre are attempts to formulate those answers which Sartre himself might give to his critics. However, we are not in agreement with all of these answers and do not think that they fully exonerate Sartre's inadequacies and weaknesses. Our basic criticism throughout this work has been that Sartre's failure to make use of true Husserlain phenomenology deprives his work of the method necessary to a successful ontological investigation. We have gone so far as to assert that this methodological failure basically invalidates Sartre's ontology. We have not attempted to answer the question which has been raised by the positivists: Is ontology a valid area of philosophic inquiry?, for an answer to this question, were it to be done adequately, would require a separate study. But in order to give some indication of what our answer might be, we may once again turn to Husserl's phenomenology and may try to see what possibilities it contains intrinsically which might qualify it as the proper instrument for ontological inquiry. Let us first see what Husserl himself has contributed to the general question of the relationship between phenomenology and metaphysics.

At first glance it might appear that Husserl's phenomenology is incommensurable with metaphysics. Since Husserl's phenomenological program is to develop a method which will make philosophy a "rigorous science," it seems that the dark tangles and confusions of metaphysics would be the first things to be eliminated from this program. Husserl says:

> "Profundity is the symptom of a chaos which true science must strive to resolve into a cosmos, i.e., into a simple, unequivocal, pellucid order. True science, insofar as it has become definable doctrine, knows no profundity. Every science, or part of a science, which has attained finality, is a coherent system of reasoning operations each of which is immediately intelligible; thus, not profound at all. Profundity is the concern of wisdom; that of methodical theory is conceptual clarity and distinctness. To reshape and transform the dark gropings of profundity into unequivocal, rational propositions: that is the essential act in methodically constituting a new science." [20]

However, our problem is the interpretation of Husserl's philosophy and its internal relationships with metaphysics. The quotation just

[20] Husserl, E., "Philosophie als strenge Wissenschaft,"; quoted and translated in "Phenomenology and Metaphysics," by Landgrebe, *Philosophy and Phenomenological Research*, Vol. X, No. 2 (December, 1949), 197.

given sets the stage for the inquiry and does not give us any sort of final answer. We must remember that phenomenological method is a propaedeutic to all disciplines and branches of philosophy, and that, therefore, it bears *some* distinct relationship to metaphysics. The first indication of what this relationship might be is given by Farber when he writes:

> "The characteristic concepts of metaphysics, such as being, reality, object, etc., are clarified in a preliminary way by being referred back to the rudimentary level of experience from which they first derive their sense." [21]

The "rudimentary level" is the level of pure consciousness divorced from the "natural attitude." It is here that the first distinction vital to comprehending the relation between phenomenology and metaphysics must be found: phenomenology is concerned with *a priori* grounds of Being as they may be grasped in the intuitions of the pure ego. Phenomenology is not concerned with metaphysics as the *a priori* analysis of Being *in general;* i.e., with an investigation of the structures of Being apart from their foundation in the content of consciousness as *intuited elements.*

> "Phenomenology is anti-metaphysical only with respect to the tradition. It attempts the construction of *a priori* sciences on the basis of concrete intuition—such sciences as pure grammar, p⸀ure logic, pure law, the eidetic science of the world intuitively apprehended, etc., and the elaboration of a general ontology of the objective world which embraces everything. This is metaphysics, says Husserl, if it is true that the ultimate knowledge of being may be called metaphysics. Rejecting the traditional metaphysics because of its speculative excesses, he sets up his own 'apodictic' theory. Eidetic descriptions of constitutive experiences take the place of physical reality." [22]

Thus, while metaphysics is admissible in so far as its foundations are phenomenologically grounded in the intuitions of consciousness, the traditional speculative metaphysics is rejected and "the problem of an *a priori* ontology of the real world, which is intended to make

---

[21] Farber, M., "Phenomenology," *op. cit.,* 363.
[22] Farber, M., *The Foundation of Phenomenology,* 533.

clear its universal structure as conforming to intuitively given essential laws, is not truly philosophical in Husserl's sense." [23]

Let us look more carefully into Husserl's rejection of speculative metaphysics. The "quest for Being" which characterizes traditional metaphysics is really a quest for the *origin* of Being. It was the contribution of Kant to show that "the origin of the whole of Being cannot be anything actually to be met with . . . as a part of the existing universe." [24] The reaction of idealism to this insight was the attempt to locate the Absolute in human subjectivity. "But the relation of the absolute, Mind, as subjectivity, to mind as human consciousness, was never fully clarified and this lack of clarity brought about the shipwreck of idealism." [25] It is at this point that phenomenology takes up the problem of Being and offers a solution by redefining the idealist principle of the dependence of experience upon the subjectivity into the phenomenological principle of the dependence of the structure of experience upon the meaning-endowing acts of consciousness.

> "The world, the totality of all Being, into whose 'origin' metaphysics inquires, is not a sum or collection of objects known and fixed from the outset, but that articulated into objects as it presents itself to us, it is but the result or function of the performances (*Leistungen*) of subjectivity, in which it constitutes itself *as* a world. Already Kant's 'categories,' no less than the Leibnizian idea of the *vis apperceptiva* of the monad, had been the first stirrings of the discovery of this *functional dependence of the world on subjectivity*." [26]

Speculative metaphysics gives way to phenomenological metaphysics, and the abstractness of speculative thought gives way to the concreteness of phenomenological intuition. In this radical sense, "metaphysics is an answer to the question of Being, of its meaning and origin, of the origin of the universe, and the absolute Being—*not* by puzzling out a dimly suspected behind-the-world, beyond all possible knowledge, but *by analyzing 'performances' and* functions of consciousness." [27]

[23] Farber, M., *The Foundation of Phenomenology*, 532.
[24] Landgrebe, *op. cit.*, 202.
[25] *Ibid.*
[26] *Ibid.*, 203.
[27] *Ibid.*, 204.

We are thus on the true terrain of Husserlian phenomenology, which offers to us the distinctive *method* for the analysis of consciousness. To pursue our problem any further would require a detailed study of phenomenology and Husserl's life-work, a task which is beyond the scope of this study. Our sole purpose in raising the question of the relationship between metaphysics and phenomenology was to show in a general way how Husserl's phenomenological method might be used in an ontological investigation. Since we brought up the problem of the relationship between metaphysics and phenomenology in regard to the positivistic attack against ontology, it is valuable to note that whatever the accomplishments and validity of the positivistic criticism of metaphysics, the positivists have not investigated the possibility of a true phenomenological ontology, and their criticisms of speculative metaphysics, therefore, have not been shown to be valid also against the Husserlian approach.

Our study of Sartre's EN leads us to conclude that the problem of Being which he investigates is a genuine philosophical problem but that his solution of this problem is fundamentally inadequate because of his failure to develop and make use of an appropriate phenomenological method. While we cannot accept Sartre's main conclusions, we must commend his efforts in raising once again vitally important philosophic issues which much of contemporary philosophy has tended to ignore or defame. Sartre's work is intimately connected with "perennial philosophy," and the questions he raises concerning man's Being, freedom, anguish, and responsibility are crucial problems which philosophy *must* attempt to clarify and answer. Sartre's shortcomings have thus prepared the way for an advance beyond quasi-phenomenological ontology. Whether or not this advance, making use of Husserl's method, will succeed, we leave an open question. Sartre's greatest achievement is to have returned us to the nexus of philosophic problems concerned with the ultimate isomorphism between human subjectivity and human reality. We are returned, then, to the profound core of Kant's Copernican revolution and to the question: Can phenomenological ontology complete or advance beyond the Copernican revolution?

APPENDIX

Appendix

All quotations from *L'Être et le Néant* have been translated from the original French by the author of this work. To date, there has been no translation of *L'Être et le Néant* into English. All other quotations from foreign languages have been translated from the original source by the author of this work with the exception of a few instances which are clearly noted in the footnotes involved.

The following French quotations are the originals from which the main quotations in this work have been taken. Each quotation is identified by the number of the page in this work on which the translation appears, and the footnote on that page which gives the reference to the original work.

Page 14, footnote 22 (Varet, G., *L'Ontologie de Sartre*, 17)
"L'échec de la critique kantienne commence avec l'idée que la théorie de la connaissance peut se faire de façon indépendante, sans une ontologie."

Page 14, footnote 23 (Varet, G., *L'Ontologie de Sartre*, 15)
"Dans l'idée critique, toute question sur *l'être* appelle l'examen des conditions pour le connaître . . . Ainsi, chez Heidegger et chez Sartre, toute question philosophique a pour propriété—c'est l'essence même d'une question philosophique—de renvoyer aux *possibles* de cette question. Dans ce sens précis, tout existentialiste conscient, phénoménologue ou non, Sartre en particulier, est largement tributaire de la 'Révolution' Kantienne, qui est bien une des acquisitions fondamentales de la philosophie moderne: ce doit être désormais le caractère distinctif de toute philosophie que d'inclure dans sa propre problématique l'entreprise philosophique dans son ensemble, et partant le philosophie lui-même."

Page 32, footnote 10 (EN, 299)
"la vérité est vérité du Tout. Et il se place du point de la verité, c'est-à-dire du Tout pour envisager le problème de l'autre. Ainsi, lorsque le monisme hégélien considère la relation des consciences, il ne se place en aucune conscience particulière. Bien que le Tout soit à réaliser, il est déjà comme la vérité de tout ce qui est vrai; aussi, lorsque Hegel écrit que toute conscience étant identique avec

elle-même est autre que l'autre, il s'est établi dans le tout, en dehors des consciences et les considère du point de vue de l'Absolu."

Page 33, footnote 11 (EN, 299)

"l'optimisme de Hegel aboutit à un échec: entre l'objet-autrui et moi-sujet, il n'y a aucune commune mesure, pas plus qu'entre la conscience (de) soi et la conscience *de* l'autre. Je ne puis pas me connaître *en* autrui si autrui est d'abord objet pour moi et je ne peux pas non plus saisir autrui dans son être vrai, c'est-à-dire dans sa subjectivité. Aucune connaissance universelle ne peut être tirée de la relation des consciences. C'est ce que nous appellerons leur séparation ontologique."

Page 39, footnote 51 (EN, 389–390)

"Nous avons renoncé à nous doter *d'abord* d'un corps pour étudier *ensuite* la façon dont nous saisissons ou modifions le monde à travers lui. Mais, au contraire, nous avons donné pour fondement au dévoilement du corps comme tel, notre relation originelle au monde, c'est-à-dire notre surgissement même au milieu de l'être. Loin que le corps soit *pour nous* premier et qu'il nous dévoile les choses, ce sont les choses-ustensiles qui, dans leur apparition originelle, nous indiquent notre corps."

Page 41, footnote 60 (EN, 413)

"ces froncements de sourcils, cette rougeur . . . qui semblent . . . menaçants n'*expriment* pas la colère, ils *sont* la colère. Mais il faut bien l'entendre: en soi-même un poing serré n'est rien et ne signifie rien. Mais aussi ne percevons-nous jamais *un poing serré*: nous percevons un homme qui, dans une certaine situation, serre le poing. Cet acte signifiant considéré en liaison avec le passé et les possibles, compris à partir de la totalité synthétique 'corps en situation,' *est* la colère."

Page 41, footnote 61 (EN, 418)

"Le corps pour autrui est l'objet magique par excellence. Ainsi, le corps d'autrui est-il toujours 'corps-plus-que-corps,' parce qu'-'autrui m'est donné sans intermediaire et totalement dans le dépassement perpétuel de sa facticité."

Page 42, footnote 62 (EN, 418–419)

"J'existe mon corps: telle est sa première dimension d'être. Mon corps est utilisé et connu par autrui: telle est sa seconde dimension.

Mais en tant que *je suis pour autrui,* autrui se dévoile à moi comme le sujet pour lequel je suis objet. Il s'agit même là, nous l'avons vu, de ma relation fondamentale avec autrui. J'existe donc pour moi comme connu par autrui—en particulier dans ma facticité même. J'existe pour moi comme connu par autrui à titre de corps. Telle est la troisième dimension ontologique de mon corps."

Page 49, footnote 9 (EN, 515)

"Être, pour le pour-soi, c'est néantiser l'en-soi qu'il est. Dans ces conditions, la liberté ne saurait être rien autre que cette néantisation. C'est par elle que le pour-soi échappe à son être comme a son essence, c'est par elle qu'il est toujours autre chose que ce qu'on peut dire de lui, car... [le pour-soi] est déjà par delà le nom qu'on lui donne, la propriété qu'on lui reconnaît. Dire que le pour-soi a à être ce qu'il est, dire qu'il est ce qu'il n'est pas en n'étant pas ce qu'il est, dire qu'en lui l'existence précède et conditionne l'essence ou . . . que pour lui 'Wesen ist was gewesen ist,' c'est dire une seule et même chose, à savoir que l'homme est libre."

Page 50, footnote 14 (EN, 569)

"A désir égal d'escalade, le rocher sera aisé à gravir pour tel ascensionniste athlétique, difficile pour tel autre, novice, mal entraîné et au corps malingre. Mais le corps ne se révèle à son tour comme bien ou mal entraîné que par rapport à un choix libre. C'est parce que je suis là et que j'ai fait de moi ce que je suis que le rocher développe par rapport à mon corps un coefficient d'adversité. Pour l'avocat demeuré à la ville et qui plaide, le corps dissimulé sous sa robe d'avocat, le rocher n'est ni difficile ni aisé à gravir: il est fondu dans la totalité 'monde' sans en émerger aucunement."

Page 51, footnote 16 (EN, 577–578)

"Examinons de plus près ce paradoxe: la liberté étant choix est changement. Elle se définit par la fin qu'elle pro-jette, c'est-a-dire par le futur qu'elle a à être. Mais, précisément parce que le futur est *l'état-qui n'est-pas-encore de ce qui est,* il ne peut se concevoir que dans une étroite liaison à ce qui est. Et ce ne saurait être ce qui est qui éclaire ce qui n'est pas encore: car ce qui est *manque* et, par suite, ne peut être connu comme tel qu'à partir de ce dont il manque."

Page 55, footnote 8 (EN, 694)

"considérerions-nous l'étude de M. Bachelard sur l'eau, qui fourmille d'aperçus ingénieux et profonds, comme un ensemble de suggestions, comme une collection précieuse de matériaux qui defraient être utilisés, à présent, par une psychanalyse consciente de ses principes."

Page 55, footnote 11 (EN, 700)

"Le visqueux est *docile*. Seulement, au moment même où je crois le posseder, voilà que, par un curieux renversement, c'est *lui* qui me possede. C'est là qu'apparaît son caractère essentiel: sa mollesse fait ventouse. L'objet que je tiens dans ma main, s'il est solide, je peux le lâcher quand il me plaît; son inertie symbolise pour moi mon entière puissance: je le fonde, mais il ne me fonde point . . . voici que le visqueux renverse les termes: le Pour-soi est soudain *compromis*. J'écarte les mains, je veux lâcher le visqueux et il adhère à moi, il me pompe, il m'aspire; son mode d'être n'est ni l'inertie reassurante du solide, ni un dynamisme comme celui de l'eau qui s'épuise à me fuir: c'est une activité molle, baveuse et féminine d'aspiration, il vit obscurément sous mes doigts et je sense comme un vertige, il m'attire . . . comme le fond d'un précipice pourrait m'attirer. Il y a comme une fascination tactile du visqueux. Je ne suis plus le maître d'*arrêter* le processus d'appropriation."

Page 58, footnote 2 (EN, 639)

"l'homme, étant condamné à être libre, porte le poids du monde tout entier sur ses epaules: il est responsable du monde et de luimême en tant que manière d'être . . . la responsabilité du pour-soi est accablante, puisqu'il est celui par qui il se fait qu'*il y ait* un monde; et, puisqu'il est aussi celui qui *se fait être,* quelle que soit donc la situation où il se trouve, le pour-soi doit assumer entièrement cette situation . . . avec la conscience orgueilleuse d'en être l'auteur . . . la situation est *mienne* . . . parce qu'elle est l'image de mon libre choix de moi-même et tout ce qu'elle me présente est *mien* en ce que cela me représer.te et me symbolise."

Page 58, footnote 4 (EN, 579)

"la signification du passé est étroitement dépendante de mon projet présent. Cela ne signifie nullement que je puis faire varier au gré de mes caprices le sens de mes actes antérieurs; mais, bien au contraire, que le projet fondamental que je suis décide absolument de la signification que peut avoir pour moi et pour les autres, le passé que j'ai à être. Moi-seul en effet peut décider à chaque moment de la *portée* du passé: non pas en discutant, en délibérant et en appréciant en chaque cas l'importance de tel ou tel événement antérieur, mais en me pro-jetant vers mes buts, je sauve le passé avec moi et je *décide* par l'action de sa signification. Cette crise mystique de ma quinzième année, qui décidera si elle 'a été' pur accident de puberté ou au contraire premier signe d'une conversion future? Moi, selon que je deciderai—à vingt ans, à trente ans—de me convertir. Le projet de conversion confère d'un seul coup à une crise d'adolescence la valeur d'une prémonition que je n'avais pas prise au sérieux."

Page 59, footnote 9 (EN, 680–681)

"dans la mesure où je m'apparais comme *créant* les objets par le seul rapport d'*appropriation*, ces objets sont *moi*. Le stylo et la pipe, le vêtement, le bureau, la maison, *c'est moi*. La totalité de mes possessions réfléchit la totalité de mon être. Je *suis* ce que j'ai. *C'est moi* que je touche sur cette tasse, sur ce bibelot. Cette montagne que je gravis, *c'est moi* dans la mesure où je la vaincs; et lorsque je suis à son sommet, que j'ai 'acquis,' au prix de mêmes efforts, ce large point de vue sur la vallée et sur les cimes environnates, je *suis* le point de vue; le panorama, c'est moi dilaté jusqu'à l'horizon, car il n'existe que par moi, que pour moi."

Page 72, footnote 28 (EN, 28)

"C'est en vain qu'on tentera un tour de passe-passe, en fondant la *réalité* de l'objet sur la plénitude subjective impressionnelle et son *objectivité* sur le non-être: jamais l'objectif ne sortira du subjectif, ni le transcendant de l'immanence, ni l'être du non-être. Mais, dira-t-on, Husserl définit précisément la conscience comme une transcendance. En effet: c'est là ce qu'il pose; et c'est sa découverte essentielle. Mais . . . il est totalement infidèle à son principe."

Page 72, footnote 29 (EN, 28)

"La conscience est conscience *de* quelque chose: cela signifie que la transcendance est structure constitutive de la conscience; c'est-à-dire que la conscience naît *portée sur* un être qui n'est pas elle. C'est ce que nous appelons la preuve ontologique."

Page 72, footnote 30 (EN, 28–29)

"Dire que la conscience est conscience de quelque chose cela signifie qu'il n'y a pas d'être pour la conscience en dehors de cette obligation précise d'être intuition révélante de quelque chose, c'est-à-dire d'un être transcendant . . . Or, une intuition révélante implique un révélé. La subjectivité absolue ne peut se constituer qu'en face d'un révélé, l'immanence ne peut se definir que dans la saisie d'un transcendant."

Page 83, footnote 20 (EN, 109)

"On *se met de* mauvaise foi comme on s'endort et on est de mauvaise foi comme on rêve. Une fois ce mode d'être réalisé, il est aussi difficile d'en sortir que de se réveiller: c'est que la mauvaise foi est un type d'être dans le monde, comme la veille ou le rêve, qui tend par lui-même à se perpétuer."

Page 84, footnote 22 (EN, 111)

"Si la mauvaise foi est possible, c'est qu'elle est la menace immédiate et permanente de tout projet de l'être humain, c'est que la conscience recèle en son être un risque permanent de mauvaise foi. Et l'origine de ce risque, c'est que la conscience, à la fois et dans son être, est ce qu'elle n'est pas et n'est pas ce qu'elle est."

Pages 87–88, footnote 24 (EN, 711–712)

"le Pour-soi et l'En-soi sont réunis par une liaison synthétique qui n'est autre que le Pour-soi lui-même. Le Pour-soi, en effet, n'est pas autre chose que la pure néantisation de l'En-soi; il est comme un trou d'être au sein de l'Être . . . Le Pour-soi n'a d'autre réalité que d'être la néantisation de l'être. Sa seule qualification lui vient de ce qu'il est néantisation de l'En-soi individuel et singulier et non d'un être en général. Le Pour-soi n'cest pas le néant en général mais une privation singulière; il se constitue en privation de *cet être-ci*."

Page 88, footnote 25 (EN, 712)

"Nous n'avons donc pas lieu de nous interroger sur la manière dont le pour-soi peut s'unir à l'en-soi puisque le pour-soi n'est aucunement une substance autonome."

Pages 88–89, footnote 26 (EN, 715–716)

"l'en-soi et le pour-soi ne sont pas juxtaposés. Bien au contraire, le pour-soi sans l'en-soi est quelque chose comme un abstrait: il ne saurait pas plus exister qu'une couleur sans forme ou qu'un son sans hauteur et sans timbre; une conscience qui ne serait conscience *de* rien serait un rien absolu."

Page 89, footnote 27 (EN, 716)
"si la conscience est liée à l'en-soi par une relation *interne,* cela ne signifie-t-il pas qu'elle s'articule avec lui pour constituer une totalité et n'est-ce pas à cette totalité que revient la dénomination d'*être* ou de réalité? Sans doute, le pour-soi est néantisation, mais, à titre de néantisation, il *est;* et il est en unité *a priori* avec l'en-soi."

Page 89, footnote 28 (EN, 716)
"si nous devions considérer l'être total comme constitué par l'organisation synthétique de l'en-soi et du pour-soi, n'allons-nous pas retrouver la difficulté que nous voulions éviter? Ce hiatus que nous décelions dans le concept d'être, n'allons-nous pas le rencontrer à présent dans l'existant lui-même?"

Page 90, footnote 31 (EN, 716–717)
"Si nous voulions concevoir une organisation synthétique telle que le pour-soi soit inséparable de l'en-soi et que, réciproquement, l'en-soi soit indissolublement liée au pour-soi, il faudrait la concevoir de telle sorte que l'en-soi reçoive son existence de la néantisation qui en fait prendre conscience. Qu'est-ce à dire sinon que la totalité indissoluble d'en-soi et de pour-soi n'est concevable que sous la forme de l'être 'cause de soi.' "

Page 90, footnote 32 (EN, 717)
"le réel est un effort avorté pour atteindre à la dignité de cause-de-soi. Tout se passe comme si le monde, l'homme et l'homme-dans-le-monde n'arrivaient à réaliser qu'un Dieu manqué. Tout se passe donc comme si l'en-soi et le pour-soi se présentaient en état de *désintégration* par rapport à une synthèse idéale. Non que l'intégration ait jamais *eu lieu,* mais précisément au contraire parce qu'elle est toujours indiquée et toujours impossible. C'est le perpétuel échec qui explique à la fois l'indissolubilité de l'en-soi et du pour-soi et leur relative indépendance."

Page 96, footnote 5 (EN, 680–681)
"La totalité de mes possessions réfléchit la totalité de mon être. Je *suis* ce que *j'ai. C'est moi* que je touche sur cette tasse, sur ce

bibelot. Cette montagne que je gravis, *c'est moi* dans la mesure où je la vaincs; et lorsque je suis à son sommet, que j'ai 'acquis,' au prix de mêmes efforts, ce large point de vue sur la vallée et sur les cimes environnantes, je *suis le* point de vue; le panorama, c'est moi dilaté jusqu'à l'horizon, car il n'existe que par moi, que pour moi."

Pages 96–97, footnote 6 (EN, 681)

"La possession est un rapport magique; je *suis* ces objets que je possède, mais dehors, face à moi; je les crée comme indépendants de moi; ce que je possède, c'est *moi hors* de moi, hors de toute subjectivité, comme un en-soi qui m'échappe à chaque instant et dont je perpétue à chaque instant la création."

Page 104, footnote 6 (EN, 152–153)

"Husserl a été, tout au long de sa carrière philosophique, hanté par l'idée de la transcendance et du dépassement. Mais les instruments philosophiques dont il disposait, en particulier sa conception idéaliste de l'existence, lui ôtaient les moyens de rendre compte de cette transcendance: son intentionnalité n'en est que la caricature. La conscience husserlienne ne peut en réalité se transcender ni vers le monde, ni vers l'avenir, ni vers le passé."

BIBLIOGRAPHY

Bibliography

PRIMARY SOURCES

A. *Jean-Paul Sartre: Philosophical Works* (in chronological order)

"Légende de la vérité," *Bifur*, 8 jun., 1931.

"La transcendance de l'ego, esquisse d'une description phénoménolgique," *Recherches Philosophiques*, 6: 1936–1937.

L'imagination, Paris, 1936.

"La structure intentionelle de l'image," *Revue de Métaphysique et de Morale*, 45: 4, Oct., 1938.

"Une idée fondamentale de la 'Phénoménoligie' de Husserl," *Nouvelle Revue Française*, 52: 304, Jan., 1939.

Esquisse d'une theorie des émotions, Paris, 1939. (English translation: *The Emotions, Outline of a Theory*, N. Y., 1948).

"M. Jean Giraudoux et la philosophie d'Aristote. A propos de 'Choix des élues'," *Nouvelle Revue Française*, 54: 318, March, 1940.

L'imaginaire, psychologie phénoménologique de l'imagination, Paris, 1940. (English translation: *The Psychology of Imagination*, N. Y., 1948).

L'Être et le Néant, essai d'ontologie phénoménologique, Paris, 1943.

"Materialisme et révolution," *Les Temps Modernes*, 1:9 June, 1946.

Descartes, (Introduction to Descartes' Work, ed. by Sartre), Paris, 1946.

L' existentialisme est un humanisme, Paris, 1946. (English translation: *Existentialism*, N. Y., 1947).

Réflexions sur la question juive, Paris, 1946. (English translation: *Anti-Semite and Jew*, N. Y., 1948).

Baudelaire, precédeé d'une note de Michel Leiris, Paris, 1947. (English translation: Baudelaire, London, 1949).

Situations I, Paris, 1947.

Situations II, Paris, 1948.

("Qu'est-ce que la litterature?," a part of *Situations II*, has been translated into English as *What is Literature?*, N. Y., 1949).

Situation III, Paris, 1949.

B. *Jean-Paul Sartre: Novels and Plays* (in chronological order)

La nausée, Paris, 1938. (English translation: *Nausea*, N. Y., 1949. "The Root of the Chestnut Tree," a chapter of *La nausée*, was especially translated for publication in *Partisan Review*, Winter, 1946).

Le mur, Paris, 1939. (English translation: *The Wall ond other stories*, N. Y., 1948).

Les mouches, Paris, 1943. (English translation: *The flies* (together with *No exit (Huis clos)*), N. Y., 1947.

Huis clos, piece en un acte, Paris, 1945.
(English translation given above).

Les Chemins de la liberté. I L'age de raison, Paris, 1945.
("Les Chemin de la liberté" is the title for a projected teralogy of which three volumes have been published in France) (English translation: *The roads to freedom. I The age of reason,* N. Y., 1947)

Les Chemins de la liberté. II Le sursis, Paris, 1945.
(English translation: *The Reprieve,* N. Y., 1947).

Theatre I, Paris, 1947.
(Contains Sartre's first four plays: Les Mouches, Huis clos, Morts sans sépulture, La Putain respecteuse). (English translations of last two plays appear in *Three Plays,* N. Y., 1949).

Les jeux sont faits, Paris, 1947.
(English translation: *The Chips are Down,* N. Y., 1948).

Les mains sales, Paris, 1948.
(English translation: *Dirty Hands,* in *Three Plays, op. cit.*).

Les Chemins de la Liberté. III La mort dans l'âme, Paris, 1949.
(English translation: *Troubled Sleep,* N. Y., 1951).

Les Chemins de la Liberté. IV La dernière chance (in preparation).

BIBLIOGRAPHIES ON SARTRE

Douglas, Kenneth, *A Critical Bibliography of Existentialism (The Paris School),* Yale French Studies Special Monograph No. 1, New Haven, Connecticut, 1950.
   Included in this bibliography is a complete listing of all of Sartre's writings, from his unpublished juvenalia to his latest interview with the press. In addition to the complete listing of all books, articles, reviews, interviews, broadcasts, etc., there is a thorough account of all books and articles which have criticized all aspects of Sartre's thought, philosophic and non-philosophic. This work represents, then, a complete bibliography of Sartre's writings and of the criticisms of Sartre's writings.

Jolivet, Régis, *Französische Existenzphilosophie,* Bern, 1948.

Yanitelli, Victor R., "A Bibliographical Introduction to Existentialism," *The Modern Schoolman,* Vol. XXVI, No. 4, May, 1949.

"Bibliographie," *Revue Internationale de Philosophie,* Troisième année, Juillet, 1939.

SECONDARY SOURCES

A. *Books*

Audry, Collette (ed.), *Pour et Contre L'existentialisme:* grand débat avec J. B. Pontalis, J. Pouillon, F. Jeanson, Julien Benda, Emm. Mounier, R. Vailland. Un texte de Jean-Paul Sartre, Paris, 1948.

Barrett, William, *What is Existentialism?,* N. Y., 1947.

Beigbeder, Marc, *L'homme Sartre: Essai de devoilement préexistentiel,* Bordas, 1947.

Benda, Julien, *Tradition de L'existentialisme,* Paris, 1947.

Bobbio, Norberto, *The Philosophy of Decadentism: A Study in Existentialism*, Oxford, 1948.

Boutang, Pierre, and Pingaud, Bernard, *Sartre, est-il un possedé?*, Paris, 1946.

Campbell, Robert, *Jean-Paul Sartre: ou une Littérature Philosophique*, Paris, 1945.

Farber, Marvin, (ed.), *Philosophic Thought in France and the United States*, Buffalo, N.Y., 1950.

Farber, Marvin, *The Foundation of Phenomenology*, Cambridge, Mass., 1943.

Foulquié, Paul, *Existentialism*, London, 1948.

Grene, Marjorie, *Dreadful Freedom*, Chicago, 1948.

Harper, Ralph, *Existentialism: A Theory of Man*, Cambridge, Mass., 1948.

Hessen, G., *Existenzphilosophie*, Basel, 1948.

Hoffman, Kurt, *Existential Philosophy: A Study of its Past and Present Forms*, Harvard University Ph.D. dissertation, March, 1949.

Husserl, Edmund, *Ideas: General Introduction to Pure Phenomenology*, London, 1931.

Husserl, Edmund, *Logische Untersuchungen*, 2 vols., 4th ed., Halle, 1928.

Husserl, Edmund, *Méditations Cartésiennes*, Paris, 1947.

Jeanson, F., *Le Problème moral et la Pensée de Sartre*, (Introduction by Sartre), Paris, 1946.

Jolivet, R., *Les Doctrines existentialistes, de Kierkegaard à J.-P. Sartre*, Paris, 1948.

Kuhn, Helmut, *Encounter With Nothingness, An Essay on Existentialism*, Hinsdale, Illinois, 1949.

Lefebvre, Henri, *L'existentialisme*, Paris, 1946.

Lukacs, Georges, *Existentialisme ou Marxisme?*, Paris, 1948.

Mounier, Emmanuel, *Existentialist Philosophies, An Introduction*, London, 1948.

Ruggiero, Guido de, *Existentialism: Disintegration of Man's Soul*, N.Y., 1948.

Troisfontaines, Roger, *Le Choix de J.-P. Sartre, exposé et critique de l'être et le néant*, Paris, 1945.

Truc, Gonzague, *De J.-P. Sartre à L. Lavella ou Desagregation et Reintegration*, Paris, 1946.

Varet, Gilbert, *L'Ontologie de Sartre*, Paris, 1948.

Wahl, Jean, *A Short History of Existentialism*, N.Y., 1949.

B. *Articles*

Alquié, F., "L'Être et le Néant, par J.-P. Sartre," *Cahiers du sud*, No. 273–274, 1945.

Arendt, Hannah, "What is Existenz Philosophy?," *Partisan Review*, Winter, 1946.

Ayer, A. J., "Novelist-Philosophers V, Jean-Paul Sartre," *Horizon*, Vol. XII, Nos. 67–68, July-August, 1945.

Beck, Maximillian, "Existentialism versus Naturalism and Idealism," *The South Atlantic Quarterly*, April, 1948, Vol. 47, No. 2.

Blondel, Maurice, "The Inconsistency of Jean-Paul Sartre's Logic," *The Thomist*, X, 1947.

Boorsch, Jean, "Sartre's View of Cartesian Liberty," *Yale French Studies*, Vol. 1, No. 1, Spring-Summer, 1948.

Campbell, Robert, "Existentialism in France since the Liberation," *Philosophic Thought in France and the United States*, (ed. by Marvin Farber), Buffalo, N. Y., 1950.

Castelli, Enrico, "L'existentialisme: philosophie de la crise," *Revue Internationale de Philosophie*, Troisième année, No. 9, Juillet, 1949.

Chenu, J., "J.–P. Sartre et L'existentialisme," *Le Monde Français*, 1946.

Cohn, Robert G., "Sartre's First Novel: *La nausée*," *Yale French Studies*, Vol. 1, No. 1, Spring-Summer, 1948.

Collins, James, "The Existentialism of Jean-Paul Sartre," *Thought*, Vol. XXIII, No. 88, March, 1948.

Cuenot, Claude, "Litterature et philosophie chez J.–P. Sartre," *Renaissances*, 1946, No. 21.

Descoqs, P., "L'atheisme de J.–P. Sartre," *Revue Philosophique*, 1946.

De Waelhens, Alphonse, "Heidegger et Sartre," *Deucalion*, 1946.

De Waelhens, Alphonse, "J.–P. Sartre, L'être et le néant," *Erasmus*, 1: 9–10, May, 1947.

De Waelhens, *Alphonse*, "Les constantes de l'existentialisme," *Revue Internationale de Philosophie*, Troisième année, No. 9, Juillet, 1949.

De Waelhens, Alphonse, "L'existentialisme de Sartre est-il un humanisme?" *Revue Philosophique de Louvain*, 44, 1946.

Doublas, K. N., "The Nature of Sartre's Existentialism," *The Virginia Quarterly Review*, April, 1947.

Fabre, Lucien, "Essentialisme et existentialisme. Le Néant de M. Sartre," *Revue de Paris*, 54:4, April, 1947.

Farber, Marvin, "Phenomenlogy," *Twentieth Century Philosophy* (edited by Dagobert D. Runes), N. Y., 1943.

Fowlie, Wallace, "Existentialist Hero: a Study of L'Age de Raison," *Yale French Studies*, Vol. 1, No. 1, Spring-Summer, 1948.

Geiger, Moritz, "An Introduction to Existential Philosophy" (edited by Herbert Spiegelberg), *Philosophy and Phenomenological Research*, Vol. III, No. 3, March, 1943.

Godet, Pierre, "Note sur L'être et le néant, de J.–P. Sartre," *Jahrbuch des Schweizerischen Philosophischen Gesellschaft*, V, 1945.

Grene, Marjorie, "Sartre's Theory of the Emotions," *Yale French Studies*, Vol. 1, No. 1, Spring-Summer, 1948.

Heinemann, F. H., "What is Alive and What is Dead in Existentialism?," *Revue Internationale de Philosophie*, Troisième année, No. 9, Juillet, 1949.

Hering, Jean, "Phenomenology in France," *Philosophic Thought in France and the United States* (edited by Marvin Farber), Buffalo, N.Y., 1950.

Husserl, Edmund, "Phenomenology," *Encyclopaedia Britannica*, 1927, 14th edition, Vol. XVII.

Jeanson, Francis, "L'existentialisme: Philosophie du sujet humain," *Pour et Contre L'Existentialisme*, Paris, 1948.

Landgrebe, Ludwig, "Phenomenology and Metaphysics," *Philosophy and Phenomenological Research*, Vol. X, No. 2, December, 1949.

Leavitt, Walter, "Sartre's Theatre," *Yale French Studies*, Vol. 1, No. 1, Spring-Summer, 1948.

Lukacs, Georg, "Existentialism," *Philosophy for the Future* (edited by Sellars, McGill, and Farber), N.Y., 1949.

McGill, V. J., "Sartre's Doctrine of Freedom," *Revue Internationale de Philosophie*, Troisième année, No. 9, Juillet, 1949.

Magny, C.-E., "Sartre ou la duplicité de l'être, Ascèse et mythomanie," *Les scandales d'Empédocle*, Neuchâtel, 1945.

Magny, C.-E., "Système de Sartre," *Esprit*, 13:4, March, 1945.

Marcuse, Herbert, "Existentialism: Remarks on Jean-Paul Sartre's L'Être et le Néant," *Philosophy and Phenomenological Research*, Vol. VIII, No. 3, March, 1948.

Merleau-Ponty, Maurice, "Jean-Paul Sartre ou un Auteur scandaleux," *Figaro littéraire*, 3. Jan., 1948.

Peyre, Henri, "Existentialism—A Literature of Despair?," *Yale French Studies*, Vol. 1, No. 1, Spring-Summer, 1948.

Picard, Gabiel, "L'Existentialisme de Jean-Paul Sartre," *Melanges de science religieuse*, III, 1946.

Polin, Raymond, "Introduction à la philosophie de J.-P. Sartre," *Revue de Paris*, LIII, 1946.

Rau, Katherine, "The Ethical Theory of Jean-Paul Sartre," *The Journal of Philosophy*, Vol. XLVI, No. 17, August 18, 1949.

Schuetz, Alfred, "Sartre's Theory of the Alter Ego," *Philosophy and Phenomenological Research*, Vol. 9, No. 2, December, 1948.

Wahl, Jean, "Essai sur le Néant d'un Problème," *Deucalion*, 1946.

Wahl, Jean, "La liberté chez Sartre," *Deucalion*, I, 1946.

Wahl, Jean, "The Present Situation and the Present Future of French Philosophy," *Philosophic Thought in France and the United States* (edited by Marvin Farber), Buffalo, N.Y., 1950.

RELATED WORKS

A. *Bibliographies and Works Containing Bibliographies*

Martin Heidegger

"Bibliographie," *Revue Internationale de Philosophie*, Troisième année, Juillet, 1949.

De Waelhens, A., *La Philosophie de Martin Heidegger*, Louvain, 1942.

Hoffman, Kurt, *Existential Philosophy: A Study of its Past and Present Forms*, Harvard University Ph.D. dissertation, March, 1949.

Yanetelli, Victor R., "A Bibliographical Introduction to Existentialism," *The Modern Schoolman*, Vol. XXVI, No. 4, May, 1949.

Edmund Husserl

Welch, E. Parl, *The Philsosophy of Edmund Husserl*, N. Y., 1941.

Karl Jaspers

"Bibliographie," *Revue Internationale de Philosophie*, Troisième année, Juillet, 1949.

Hoffman, Kurt, *Existential Philosophy: A Study of its Past and Present Forms*, Harvard University Ph.D. dissertation, March 1949.

Yanetelli, Victor R., "A Bibliographical Introduction to Existentialism," *The Modern Schoolman*, Vol. XXVI, No. 4, May, 1949.

Søren Kierkegaard

Jolivet, Régis, *Kierkegaard*, Bibliographische Einführungen in das Studium der Philosophie, Bern, 1948.

Mesnard, Pierre, *Le Vrai Visage de Kierkegaard*, Bibliotheque des Archives de Philosophie, Paris, 1948.

Yanetelli, Victor R., "A Bibliographical Introduction to Existentialism," *The Modern Schoolman*, Vol. XXVI, No. 4, May, 1949.

Gabriel Marcel

"Bibliographie," *Revue Internationale de Philosophie*, Troisième année, Juillet, 1949.

Jolivet, Régis, *Franzöische Existenzphilosophie*, Bern, 1948.

Yanetelli, Victor R., "A Bibliographical Introduction to Existentialism," *The Modern Schoolman*, Vol. XXVI, no. 4, May, 1949.

Lesser Known Existentialists: Georges Bataille, Nicolas Berdiaeff, Albert Camus, Simone de Beauvoir, and Maurice Merleau-Ponty.

Douglas, Kenneth, *A Critical Bibliography of Existentialism (The Paris School)*, Yale French Studies Special Monograph No. 1, New Haven, Connecticut, 1950.

Jolivet, Régis, *Französische Existenzphilosophie*, Bern, 1948.

Italian Existentialism

"Bibliographie," *Revue Internationale de Philosophie*, Troisième année, Juillet, 1949.

L'Archivio di Filosofia, (Organo del R. Istituto di Studi Filosofici), Roma, anno XV, vol. I e II, 1946.

B. *Books*

Ayer, A. J., *Language, Truth and Logic*, London, 1949.

Berdiaeff, Nicolas, *Cinq Méditations sur L'Existence*, Paris, 1936.

Bocheński, I. M., *Europäische Philosophie der Gegenwart*, Bern, 1947.

Brock, Werner, *An Introduction to Contemporary German Philosophy*, Cambridge, England, 1935.

Brunner, Auguste, *La Personne Incarnée: étude sur la phénoménologie et la philsophie existentialiste*, Paris, 1947.

Buber, Martin, *Between Man and Man*, N. Y., 1948.

Camus, Albert, *The Plague*, N.Y., 1948.

de Beauvoir, Simone, *L'Existentialisme et la Sagesse des Nations*, Paris, 1948.

de Beauvoir, Simone, *The Ethics of Ambiguity*, N. Y., 1948.

De Waelhens, A., *La Philosophie de Martin Heidegger*, Louvain, 1942.

Dufrenne, Mikel and Ricoeur, Paul, *Karl Jaspers et la Philosophie de l'existence*, Paris, 1947.

Farber, Marvin (ed.), *Philosophical Essays in Memory of Edmund Husserl*, Cambridge, Mass., 1940.

Gurvitch, Georges, *Les Tendances Actuelles de la Philosophie Allemande*, Paris, 1949.

Hegel, G. W. F., *The Phenomenlogy of Mind*, London, 1931.

Heidegger, Martin, *De L'Essence de la Verité*, Paris, 1948.

Heidegger, Martin, *Existence and Being*, London, 1949.

Heidegger, Martin, *Sein und Zeit*, Halle, 1927.

Jaspers, Karl, *The Perennial Scope of Philosophy*, N. Y., 1949.

Kafka, Franz, *The Trial*, N. Y., 1945.

Kierkegaard, Søren, *Fear and Trembling*, Princeton, 1941.

Laird, John, *Recent Philosophy*, London, 1945.

Levinas, Emmanuel, *Le Choix, le Monde, L'Existence*, Paris, 1948.

Levinas, Emmanuel, *De L'existence à l'existant*, Paris, 1947.

Levinas, Emmanuel, *En découvrant l'existence avec Husserl et Heidegger*, Paris, 1949.

Marcel, Gabriel, *Being and Having*, Westminster, England, 1949.

Marcel, Gabriel, *Homo Viator*, Aubier, Editions Montaigne, 1944.

Marcel, Gabriel, *The Philosophy of Existence*, N. Y., 1949.

Maritain, Jacques, *Existence and the Existant*, N. Y., 1948.

Pap, Arthur, *Elements of Analytic Philosophy*, N. Y., 1949.

Pascal, Blaise, *Pensées*, N. Y., 1941.

Tonquedec, Joseph de, *L'Existence d'après Karl Jaspers*, Paris, 1945.

Unamuno, Miguel, *Perplexities and Paradoxes*, N. Y., 1945.

Van Molle, Germaine, *La Connaissance dialectique et l'Experience existentielle*, Bibliotheque Scientifique Belge, Georges Thone (ed.), Liege, (no date).

Villaseñor, José Sánchez, *Ortega y Gasset, Existentialist*, Hinsdale, Illinois, 1949.

Wahl, Jean, *Existence Humaine et Transcendance*, Éditions de la Baconnière, Neuchatel, 1944.

Wahl, Jean, *Études Kierkegardiennes*, Paris, 1938.

Welch, E. Parl, *The Philosophy of Edmund Husserl: The Origin and Development of His Phenomenlogy*, N. Y., 1941.

C. *Articles*

Abbagnano, Nicola, "Outline of a Philosophy of Existence," *Philosophy and Phenomenological Research*, Vol. IX, No. 2, December, 1949.

Berger, Gaston, "Experience and Transcendance," *Philosophic Thought in France and the United States* (edited by Marvin Farber) , Buffalo, N. Y., 1950.

Blackham, H. J., "Karl Jaspers' Philosophy of Existence," *The Plain View*, No. 3, Vol. IV, Winter, 1949.

Blanchard, P., "L'existentialisme athée et la Morale," *Chronique sociale de France*, 1946.

Bollnow, O. Fr., "Deutsche Existenzphilosophie und französischer Existentialismus," *Zeitschrift f. phil. Forschung*, 2, 1948.

Brock, Werner, "An Account of 'Being and Time' " in *Existence and Being* by Martin Heidegger, London, 1949.

Brown, J. L., "Chief Prophet of the Existentialists," *The New York Times Magazine*, Feb. 2, 1947.

Bruneau, Jean, "Existentialism and the American Novel," *Yale French Studies*, Vol. 1, No. 1, Spring-Summer, 1948.

Brunner, A., "Zur Freiheit verurteilt," *Stimmen der Zeit*, Vol. 140, 1947.

Cassirer, Ernst, "Kant und das Problem der Metaphysik," *Kantstudien*, 1931.

Copleston, Frederick, "Existentialism and Religion," *The Dublin Review*, Spring, 1947.

Copleston, Frederick, "The Philosophy of the Absurd," *The Month*, CLXXXIV, 1947.

Copleston, Frederick, "What is Existentialism?," *The Month*, CLXXXIII, 1947.

Cornu, Auguste, "Bergsonianism and Existentialism," *Philosophic Thought in France and the United States* (edited by Marvin Farber), Buffalo, N. Y., 1950.

De Corte, M., "Réflexions sur G. Marcel et J.–P. Sartre," *Revue Philosophique*, 1946.

Dieckmann, Herbert, "French Existentialism before Sartre," *Yale French Studies*, Vol. 1, No. 1, Spring-Summer, 1948.

Dumery, Henry, "Catholic Philosophy in France," *Philosophic Thought in France and the United States* (edited by Marvin Farber), Buffalo, N. Y., 1950.

Farber, Marvin, "Descriptive Philosophy and the Nature of Human Existence," *Philosophic Thought in France and the United States* (edited by Marvin Farber), Buffalo, N. Y., 1950.

Farber, Marvin, "Experience and Subjectivism," *Philosophy for the Future* (edited by Sellars, McGill, and Farber), N. Y., 1949.

Farber, Marvin, "Professor Reulet on 'Being, Value, and Existence'," *Philosophy and Phenomenlogical Research*, Vol. X, No. 1, September, 1949.

Gascoyne, David, "Leon Chestov," *Horizon*, Vol. XX, No. 118, October, 1949.

Gérard, Jacques, "Existence et position," *Revue Internationale de Philosophie,* Troisième année, No. 9, Juillet, 1949.

Glicksman, Marjorie, "A Note on the Philosophy of Heidegger," *The Journal of Philosophy,* Vol. XXXV, No. 4, February 17, 1938.

Hartmann, Nicolai, "German Philosophy in the last Ten Years," *Mind,* Vol. LVIII, No. 232.

Havet, Jacques, "French Philosophical Tradition Between the Two Wars," *Philosophic Thought in France and the United States* (edited by Marvin Farber), Buffalo, N. Y., 1950.

Hill, E. F. F., "The Philosophy of Martin Heidegger," *World Review,* November, 1949.

Kaufman, Fritz, "Cassirer, Neo-Kantianism, and Phenomenology," *The Philosophy of Ernst Cassirer* (edited by Paul Arthur Schilpp), Evanston, Illinois, 1949.

Kecskemeti, Paul, "Existentialism: a new trend in philosophy," *New Directions 10,* N. Y., 1948.

Lavelle, Louis, "The Three Stages of Metaphysics," *Philosophic Thought in France and the United States* (edited by Marvin Farber), Buffalo, N. Y., 1950.

Lefebvre, Henri, "Knowledge and Social Criticism," *Philosophic Thought in France and the United States* (edited by Marvin Farber), Buffalo, N. Y., 1950.

Le Senne, René, "La Philosophie de L'Esprit," *Philosophic Thought in France and the United States* (edited by Marvin Farber), Buffalo, N. Y., 1950.

Magny, C.-E., "Les Chemins de la liberté," *Poesie* 45, 1945.

McKeon, Richard, "An American Reaction to the Present Situation in French Philosophy," *Philosophic Thought in France and the United States* (edited by Marvin Farber), Buffalo, N. Y., 1950.

Mehl, Roger, "The Situation of Religious Philosophy in France," *Philosophic Thought in France and the United States* (edited by Marvin Farber), Buffalo, N. Y., 1950.

Nadler, K., "Die französische Existenzphilosophie der Gegenwart," *Die Tatwelt,* Sept., 1936.

Natanson, Maurice, "H. B. Alexander's Projection of a Categoriology," *Philosophy and Phenomenological Research,* Vol. X, No. 2, December, 1949.

Natanson, Maurice, "The Prison of Being," *Prairie Schooner,* Fall, 1949.

Patrie, A., "Sur une nouvelle doctrine de la liberté," *Deucalion,* I, 1946.

Pessis, B., "In the Cesspool of Existentialism," *Soviet Literature,* Moscow, 1949.

Petrement, Simone, "La Liberté selon Descartes et selon Sartre," *Critique,* I, 1946.

Peyre, Henri, "Literature and Philosophy in Contemporary France," *Ideological Differences and World Order* (edited by F. S. C. Northrop), New Haven, Conn., 1949.

Polin, Raymond, "The Philosophy of Values in France," *Philosophic Thought in France and the United States* (edited by Marvin Farber), Buffalo, N. Y., 1950.

Pos, H. J., "L'existentialisme dans la perspective de l'historie," *Revue Internationale de Philosophie*, Troisième année, No. 9, Juillet, 1949.

Reulet, Aníbal Sánchez, "Being, Value, and Existence," *Philosophy and Phenomenological Research*, Vol. IX, No. 3, March, 1949.

Reulet, Aníbal Sánchez, "Reply to Marvin Farber," *Philosophy and Phenomenological Research*, Vol. X, No. 1, September, 1949.

Ritchie, A. M., "Language, Logic, and Existentialism," *Philosophy and Phenomenological Research*, Vol. X, No. 3, March, 1950.

Robert, J. D., "La Vie de L'Existentialisme en France," *Tijdschrift voor Philosophie*, IX, 1947.

Segond, J., "Réflexions critique sur L'existentialisme et le monde des valeurs," *Revue Internationale de Philosophie*, Troisième année, No. 9, Juillet, 1949.

Slochower, Harry, "The Function of Myth in Existentialism," *Yale French Studies*, Vol. 1, No. 1, Spring-Summer, 1948.

Smith, Vincent Edward, "Philosopher of the Absurd," *The Shield*, XXVI, 1946.

Vial, Fernand, "Existentialism and Humanism," *Thought*, XXIII, 1948.

Wahl, Jean, "Freedom and Existence in Some Recent Philosophies," *Philosophy and Phenomenological Research*, Vol. VIII, No. 4, June, 1948.

Waters, Bruce, "Existentialism in Contemporary Literature," *Prairie Schooner*, Spring, 1950.

Weiss, Paul, "Existenz and Hegel," *Philosophy and Phenomenological Research*, Vol. VIII, No. 2, December, 1947.

Werkmeister, W. H., "An Introduction to Heidegger's Existential Philosophy," *Philosophy and Phenomenological Research*, Vol. II, No. 1, September, 1941.